SECRET HOT SPRINGS

A Guide to the Weird, Wonderful, and Obscure

Cassidy Kendall

Reedy Press
PO Box 5131
St. Louis, MO 63139
reedypress.com

Library of Congress Control Number: 2024949385
ISBN: 9781681065595

Design by Jill Halpin

Unless otherwise indicated, all photos are courtesy of the author or in the public domain.

We (the publisher and the author) have done our best to provide the most accurate information available when this book was completed. However, we make no warranty, guarantee, or promise about the accuracy, completeness, or currency of the information provided, and we expressly disclaim all warranties, express or implied. Please note that attractions, company names, addresses, websites, and phone numbers are subject to change or closure, and this is outside of our control. We are not responsible for any loss, damage, injury, or inconvenience that may occur due to the use of this book. When exploring new destinations, please do your homework before you go. You are responsible for your own safety and health when using this book.

Printed in the United States of America
25 26 27 28 29   5 4 3 2 1

Dedicated to Liz Robbins and the Garland County Historical Society

Racing Tubs
Photo courtesy of Visit Hot Springs

CONTENTS

Fine Dining and Breathing
Photo courtesy of Oaklawn Racing Casino Resort

ACKNOWLEDGMENTS

This book would not have been possible without the hard work of the Garland County Historical Society, a group of volunteers whose dedication to truth, accuracy, and preservation is what keeps Hot Springs honest. I would like to give a special thanks to Liz Robbins, who graciously fact-checked and edited a large portion of the book you're holding, and to Reedy Press for giving me an opportunity to share more of Hot Springs with the world.

This work is in loving memory of our natives, Orval Allbritton, Clay Farrar, Mike Dugan, Gilbert Harris, Cooper Jack, Violet Boles, and the buffalo.

Let's Get Salty

INTRODUCTION

From the roaring era of illegal gambling that brought the most prominent gangsters in America's history to vacation, live, play, and sometimes even hide in Hot Springs, Arkansas, discover the hidden secrets of America's Spa City through colorful tales that have shaped this eccentric Southern town. Dive into the stories of madams who presided over brothels, illegal gambling rings sanctioned by local law enforcement, and the tumultuous history of the Black community, from harrowing lynchings to resilient political activism.

Learn of the city's consistent struggle against bizarre natural disasters like fires, floods, and landslides that threaten its very existence. Uncover the legacy of the thermal spring water people once traveled to from all around the world prior to modern medicine, and learn if these coveted waters flowing from Hot Springs National Park will ever run cold.

Amid the aforementioned illicit affairs and Mother Nature's relentless wrath lies a community's resilient spirit. Explore the rise of thriving businesses, from traditional staples like an alligator farm to innovative ventures like a sake brewery. Journey through the vibrant art scene, where public murals hold much more than what meets the eye, and decipher truth versus tale when it comes to the land's natives.

Prepare to be stunned by stories of cats trained on Bathhouse Row to spy on the Soviets during the cold war, and and the local who walked 8,000 miles on foot across America with his pack pony and dog. Along with infamous gangsters like Al Capone, encounter surprising connections to figures like Helen Keller, Guy Lombardo, Babe Ruth, and President Bill Clinton, each leaving their mark on Hot Springs's legacy.

Secret Hot Springs is a collage of history, mystery, and eccentricity, inviting readers to explore Hot Springs's past and get a glimpse of the secrets that lie beneath the sparkling facade that continues to draw in tourists today.

THE DOCTOR'S OUT

What is that big, abandoned building looming over downtown?

The old Army and Navy General Hospital can be seen for miles down Central Avenue before you enter downtown. The massive seven-story structure protruding from Hot Springs Mountain has been fully abandoned since 2019 and is a delicious site for history buffs.

Originally built in January 1887, the 30-bed facility was the first general hospital in the country that treated both Army and Navy patients. The government approved $100,000 for its construction, which amounts to more than $3 million today.

It was rebuilt in the early 1930s at a cost equivalent to $36 million today, reopening in 1933. The grand structure then held 400 to 600 beds and was completed just six years prior to the start of World War II, which is when the hospital peaked. During and after the war, the hospital overflowed with patients. Local hotels like the Arlington and Majestic housed soldiers the hospital campus couldn't. The Eastman Hotel, a popular 1920s lodging spot for baseball greats like Babe Ruth, was located across Reserve Street from the hospital. It was purchased to house staff and expand capacity, accommodating 700 additional patients.

READ UP ON IT

WHAT: You can see only a portion of the exterior of the abandoned hospital that sits on private property, but the Bathhouse Row Emporium directly below it has rotating literature, much of which address the structure.

WHERE: Lamar Bathhouse, 515 Central Ave.

COST: *Images of America: Hot Springs National Park* by Mary Bell Hill is sold in the emporium.

PRO TIP: Hike the Oertel Trail, located off the Promenade, to get a better view of the hospital's campus.

World War II ended in 1945, and by 1949, the hospital was called to cease operations by the secretary of defense due to high expenses. Reluctant to close, the hospital administrators held on as long as they could, closing the hospital's doors in 1955. The closure lasted only 84 days before the hospital was reopened on a much smaller scale that included 75 beds, eight doctors, and 16 nurses. Unfortunately, the hospital was still too expensive to maintain.

For four years, ideas for different uses of the facility were tossed around, and in 1959 it was decided it would become a rehabilitation center. Leased by Arkansas from the secretary of the army, in 1961 the Arkansas Rehabilitation Center occupied the building. Over the next several decades, the center would become more vocational than medical, and in 2009 it was rebranded as the Arkansas Career Training Institute (ACTI). Much of the main building was not in use, and after continuing to white-knuckle a small operation on such a grand campus, in 2019 ACTI workers were notified the institute would be closing. Shortly thereafter the building was abandoned and has remained that way ever since.

Mirroring its history, uses for the building continue to be suggested, but the expensive upkeep of such a massive structure keeps it abandoned.

LUNCH WITH LINCOLN

Can you spot Abraham Lincoln in Cafe 1217?

Cafe 1217 has been feeding Hot Springs fresh, delicious food since 1997. I have frequented this popular local restaurant for my entire life. I ate there while on vacation in Hot Springs growing up, to it becoming a regular favorite when I took up a permanent residence in Hot Springs as an adult. So when old Abe was pointed out to me by the owner a few years ago, I was shocked I had never notice him before, given that the cafe isn't that big and Lincoln is in plain sight.

This *Where's Waldo?* element is something I had never seen before. Since spotting it that day, it's something I can't unsee when I go to the restaurant. I knew this hidden Lincoln would make for a fun secret to share in this book, so I called Harris for more information. To my surprise, the story of this Lincoln was much more than a mere quirky interior design decision.

There was once a man named Bobby Geiger who made his career and local reputation at Oaklawn Racing Casino Resort's Jockey Club. Geiger was good friends with a local painter named Mark Davis, who was commissioned to paint the café's faux brick wall right around the same time Geiger's son, Landon, was learning about Abraham Lincoln in school. One thing led to another, and while taking on the painting project Davis was inspired by Landon to include a subtle portrait of Lincoln in one of the bricks. Lincoln is located on

---

Geiger's son Landon happened to be doing a paper at school on Lincoln at the time Davis asked for inspiration. It was kismet, because Lincoln just so happened to be Geiger's favorite president.

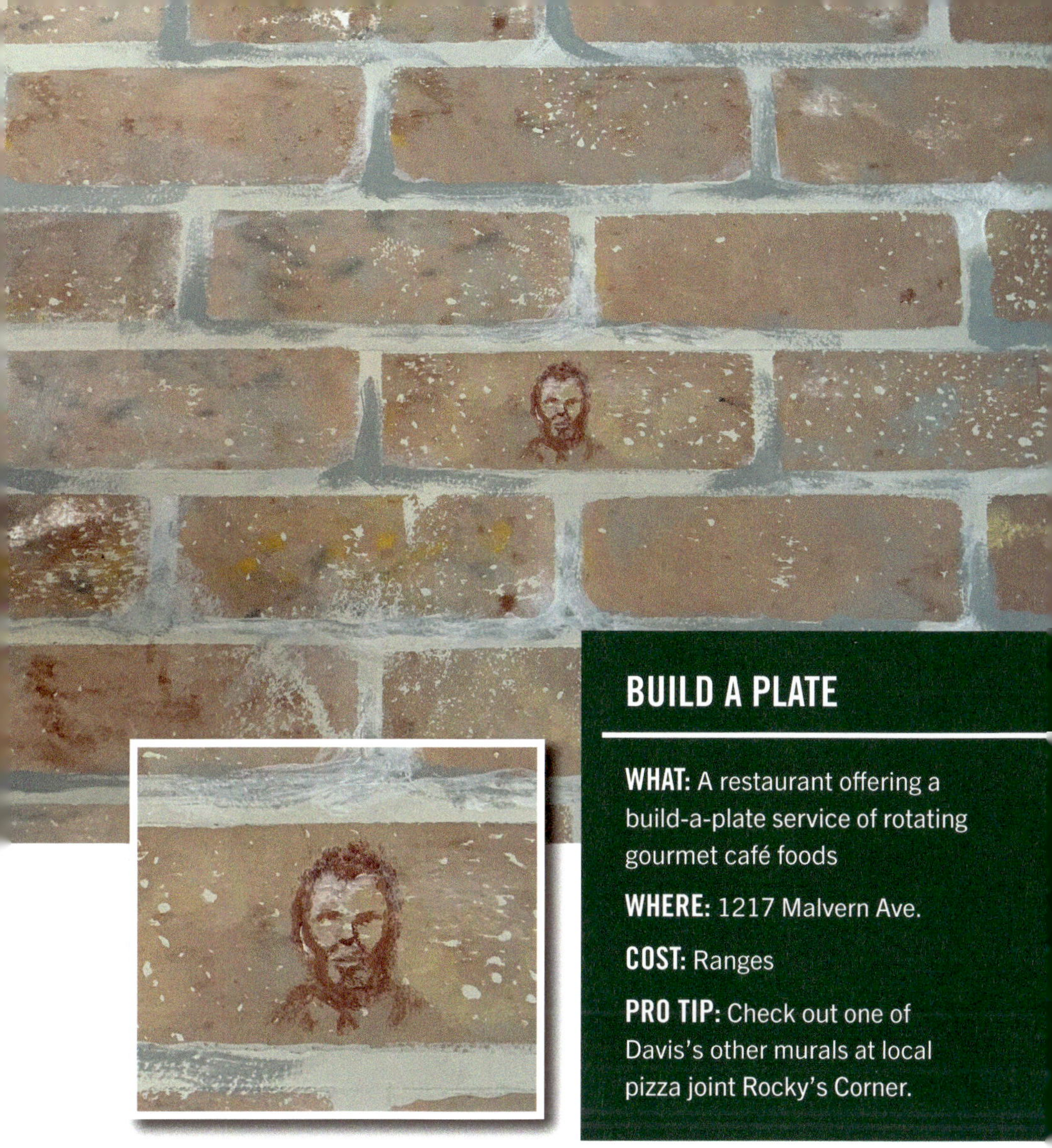

Photo courtesy of Cafe 1217

BUILD A PLATE

WHAT: A restaurant offering a build-a-plate service of rotating gourmet café foods

WHERE: 1217 Malvern Ave.

COST: Ranges

PRO TIP: Check out one of Davis's other murals at local pizza joint Rocky's Corner.

the wall above a table to your right as you enter the restaurant. When Geiger passed away in 2018 from Lou Gehrig's disease, the café dedicated the table to him.

BABE HITS HOME

Did Babe Ruth hit baseball's first-ever 500-foot home run in Hot Springs?

Hot Springs has a history of major and Negro League baseball teams coming here from around the country. From 1886 to the 1940s, Hot Springs had nearly everything these players needed: fields for playing, mountains for exercising, and thermal water therapy to heal their sore bodies. (And in some cases, the precarious activities of gambling and partying were an added bonus for these young men.)

Hot Springs attracted baseball greats like Honus Wagner, Jackie Robinson, Hank Aaron, and even the most famous baseball player of all time: Babe Ruth. It's said that Ruth, who was most famous for his home runs, hit a ball more than 500 feet during the spring of 1918 at Hot Springs's Whittington Park—something only a few players have accomplished throughout history.

With no official record of Ruth's famous hit actually happening in Hot Springs, it's greatly debated if the story is true—yet favored—and it would have likely been baseball's first 500-foot home run. Ruth's capability of completing such a feat as a rookie Red Socks pitcher in Hot Springs seems even more believable because it was recorded the following spring that Ruth hit a 587-foot home run in Tampa, Florida.

Today, this story along with many others is preserved in Hot Springs with the Historic Baseball Trail. This immersive

BABE IN ALL HIS GLORY

WHAT: Eight-foot-tall bronze statue of Ruth

WHERE: Majestic Park, 105 W Belding St.

COST: Free

PRO TIP: Visit one of three Babe Ruth statues in the world at Majestic Park when a few games are playing at its newly built five-field complex. Grab a hot dog from the concession stand and enjoy the games. Check the game schedule at majesticpark.org.

Photos courtesy of Garland County Historical Society

walking trail through downtown Hot Springs allows you to step into the past as it marks the places where famous baseball legends trained, relaxed, slept, and ate during their times in Hot Springs.

Although Hot Springs was a great destination for spring training in the beginning, it was unable to host more than a few teams a year. As time went on, teams migrated to larger areas in Florida and Arizona.

MERMAN

Is the Alligator Farm hiding a real merman?

Mermaids and mermen are creatures read about in mythology and watched on television. As far as their existence goes, some may say it's up for interpretation. The simple question *Are they real?* does not have a simple answer. It's actually met with a slew of other questions. Determining what makes a mermaid "real" is anyone's best guess. Are they part human, part fish? If so, how human are they?

MEET MERMAN

WHAT: Glass-encased merman fossil

WHERE: 847 Whittington Ave.

COST: Fee for admission, kids 0–2 free

PRO TIP: Don't let all this talk of mermen detract from the other equally cool stuff the Alligator Farm has to offer. Feed and pet alligators, goats, donkeys, bunnies, and more. There are even a few monkeys and wolves for viewing.

Are they human enough to grow long, reddish-brown locs and sing under the sea, or are they more like creatures that somewhat resemble humans but are clearly less evolved on the evolutionary scale? Or perhaps all of these questions are a moot point, and the question we should all be asking is, *Is "are" the correct tense, or is it "were"?* Some believe the reason mermaids have never been discovered is that they are extinct and therefore their existence can't be proven.

But what about dinosaurs? They are extinct and we believe in them because we have their fossils—*cough, along with a heaping pile of other archaeological evidence, cough*. You really can't discount a mermaid's existence if there is a fossil,

---

The existence of Ripley's letter poses one final question for those looking to meet Merman: *Do you believe it . . . or not?*

can you? And at the Arkansas Alligator Farm & Petting Zoo, you can find one. It's kind of on the nose, but his name is Merman. Sure, there's no science backing up his existence, but there are a lot of yellowed (surely fact-checked) newspaper clippings decorating the farm's gift shop wall "proving" his discovery.

Regardless of this undeniably ugly creature's actual origin story (be it from the China Sea, as claimed, or a faux taxidermy atrocity from someone's basement, as speculated), it has been an effective attention-grabbing gimmick for the Alligator Farm since its opening in 1902.

There is even a typewritten letter allegedly from LeRoy Robert Ripley to the Hot Springs National Park superintendent, dated June 20, 1933. In this letter displayed at the farm, Mr. Ripley requests Merman be obtained for his *Ripley's Believe It or Not! Odditorium* exhibit at the world's fair that year.

RACING TUBS

Why are bathtubs being raced down Central Avenue?

Described as a "chaotic celebration of Hot Springs' spa history," the annual Stueart Pennington's World Championship Running of the Tubs has been ruthlessly pitting groups of goofballs racing bathtubs on wheels against one another since 2006. It's one of the most entertaining and accurate depictions of the whimsy that defines the Hot Springs community.

Here's how it works: During the race, a "driver" stays in a full tub while four "bath attendants" push, holding soap, a bath mat, a loofah mitt, or a towel. Attendees squirt them with Super Soakers as they race, and bathrobed judges may create new rules along the way. The winning team reaches the finish line first with at least 10 gallons of water in the tub and attendants still holding their items.

Sounds absurd, right? It's one of the quirkiest, most creative events I have ever seen, and quite honestly completely unhinged in the spirit of competition. But none of this has answered the question, *Why do we do this?*

Hot Springs has marketed its thermal water springs for therapeutic soaking in bathhouses since the late 1800s. Hence Hot Springs's nickname, Spa City. Downtown's Bathhouse Row has been a huge economic driver for the town throughout history, but so was illegal gambling. When the gambling was mostly eradicated in 1967, the baths weren't enough to keep people coming in droves. Business no longer came as easily to downtown merchants, and the economy suffered.

Today, Running of the Tubs brings thousands to downtown Hot Springs every June and has become one of the most iconic local traditions.

In the early 2000s, one merchant thought up an idea that celebrates the local history but is absurd enough to grab the attention of the masses. His name was Stueart Pennington, and his idea was racing bathtubs in the street. The unconventional idea was met with skepticism, and unfortunately, Pennington passed away from a heart attack before he got to see his idea come to life. If he were still around today, he would see that his idea was just crazy enough to work.

SOAK A RACER

WHAT: Attend the World Championship Running of the Tubs in June, and squirt contestants with a Super Soaker.

WHERE: 500 block of Central Ave.

COST: Free

PRO TIP: Want to really get in the spirit? Wear a bathrobe, shower cap, and slippers. You won't be the only one.

Photos courtesy of Visit Hot Springs

HELL'S HALF ACRE

Is there really a pit to hell hidden in Hot Springs?

"When a terrible dragon named Mogmothon was defeated by all the forces of Heaven and thrown into the dungeons of Hell beneath Hot Springs Mountain, Mogmothon continued to struggle against the boulders that imprisoned him. He made the earth tremble with the furious thrashing of his mighty tail. His fiery breath bellowed with rage, heating the entire mountain so that nothing could grow on it.

"A Great Spirit named Gitchee Manitou feared that the peaceful valley he had set aside for the healing of his people would be destroyed by the dragon. Instead of being healed in the magic waters, the people might be consumed by sulfurous vapors and fire. Therefore, on the mountain adjacent to the Mountain of Hot Springs, he cut a vent that reached the very depths of the hell in which the dragon was trapped. Through this vent, the evil vapors spewed forth by the dragon would escape without harming the Native Americans who gathered in the sacred valley. Thus the people were saved, but they did not go near Hell's Half Acre where the groans of the dragon and his evil spirits could always be heard."

TOUR HELL'S HALF ACRE

WHAT: Take a virtual tour of what is now private property.

WHERE: YouTube: "Hell's Half Acre Tour" by Adamazide

COST: Free

PRO TIP: Vintage postcards of the site as a tourist attraction can be purchased on eBay.

This is the legend of Hot Springs's very own Hell's Half Acre from the *Indian Folklore Atlas*. The site exists and has historically been marketed as a tourist attraction. It's about 12 acres of sandstone where no greenery grows, unlike the area surrounding its borders. It has long been described as a "geographical phenomena." Now that Hell's Half Acre is

Photo courtesy of Garland County Historical Society

private property and no longer accessible to the public, what was once considered a popular picnic site has gained mystique over the years. Thanks to Jeff Gurtman of TLC's *Seeing Vs Believing* shedding light on the site as "hell's front gate" in 2010, and more recently TikTok explorers sharing footage of the desolate area, the site has been dubbed a "pit to hell" in recent years.

"For decades, two legends were associated with Hell's Half Acre—that Indians who quarried the area created the residue and that volcanic activity caused the unique rock formation," Isabel Anthony writes in *Garland County, Arkansas: Our History and Heritage*. "Hell's Half Acre was actually created several thousand years ago by one or more massive landslides of a sedimentary stratigraphic unit known as Hot Springs sandstone."

Some attribute the site to nothing more than a geographical phenomena, while Jeff Gurtman of TLC's *Seeing Vs Believing* doubled down on the lore when telling the *Sentinel-Record* on May 1, 2010, "There is certainly something going on there."

MAGNET HILL

Is there an undocumented street that will pull your parked car uphill?

Magnet Hill, located off Park Avenue, is a more recent local legend told by local broadcast journalist John Cooksey.

Cooksey, an independent journalist who has a knack for uncovering attention-grabbing stories, published a video to his YouTube channel Hot Springs Broadcast Network in December 2018, revealing his find.

"I've always loved crazy stuff on YouTube, especially things like gravity hills where cars appear to magically go uphill with no power from the car," Cooksey says in the opening of the video titled "Crazy Hot Springs street where your car seems to go uphill all by itself Gravity Hill." "I never gave it much thought in the town of Hot Springs until I drove by an empty, abandoned road with a sign on it that got me to thinking."

The street sign read "Magnet."

"The road seemed pretty level and there was not a soul on it. I was curious by that street name and I felt pulled to go there and see what would happen." In the video, you can see what appears to be Cooksey's vehicle moving forward while in neutral. "I went home to look up the street on Google Maps, and it wasn't even there," he says.

As of the publishing of this book, Magnet Street is still not shown on Google Maps. In Cooksey's video, you can see trees on both sides of the road. When I went to look at the area in 2024, all the trees on the left side of the road had been cut

TRY IT YOURSELF

WHAT: See if your car can make it up the hill.

WHERE: Take Blade St. to Cedar Glades Rd. Before you get to Cedar Glades, Magnet St. will be on your right.

COST: Free

PRO TIP: You will want to be facing toward Blade St.

down, and houses were present. I tried a few times to get my large SUV to move while in neutral. From a completely parked position, it didn't move. However, if I pressed on the gas lightly for just a moment, my car crept up the hill at a slow speed. Is it magic? Is it baloney? Or is it an optical illusion of a downhill slope appearing to be an uphill slope? My money would be on the last one. But who's to say?

> "For some magical reason, it doesn't seem to work as well with the trees cut down on one side."—John Cooksey, 2023.

LIEN AND LIEN

Who are the Liens behind Bailey's window?

Bailey's Dairy Treat is a small landmark in the Hot Springs community, serving up incredible burgers alongside a variety of Asian cuisine. The building resembles a shack that anyone unknowing would just see for its dated neon sign reading "BAILEY'S" in Arial font and the wooden paint-peeled ice cream cone atop. However, it was considered modern architecture when it was built in 1952, and it was added to the National Register of Historic Places in 2004.

"Slick lines, rounded corners, neon lighting, stucco wall finish, and corner windows emphasized the 'streamlined' look of modern design," Isabel Anthony writes in *Garland County, Arkansas: Our History and Heritage*.

Bailey's originally started out as Butchie's at 534 Park Avenue, it originally started out as Butchie's Drive-In. Before the late-1950s construction of Highway 70 entering Hot Springs on Grand Avenue, the main entry point into Hot Springs for travelers from Little Rock seeking thermal water healing or other local attractions was Highway 7, which came into town on Park Avenue. This created good business for Butchie's.

There are scarce records of the establishment, but it's known to have had multiple owners and names.

Lien Morphew, a Vietnam native, was adopted by a Hot Springs family in 1975 at the age of 15. He attended Hot Springs High School, moving to Houston after graduation. In Houston, Morphew owned a restaurant called Jade Dragon. In 1992, he married Kieulien (also known as Lien), the sister of his mom's best friend. In 1996, the two purchased Bailey's.

"Hot Springs community is very good. . . . Treat them just like family."—Lien Morphew, 2024.

STUFF YOUR FACE

WHAT: Dine out at Bailey's.

WHERE: 510 Park Ave.

COST: Ranges

PRO TIP: Trade the drink for a milkshake. Thank me later.

Creating a recipe of their own for burger patties that has stood the test of time, the two run Bailey's, successfully building it up alongside the rest of the Park Avenue neighborhood. In addition to being parents of three boys and successful business owners, the Morphews love their community and are always looking for a way to show it. In December 2021, when 71 tornadoes tore through Arkansas and other Southern states, the business donated 100 percent of its sales made on New Year's Eve to the storms' victims.

MAMOO

Who was "Mamoo" Tadlock?

Matthew "Mamoo" Tadlock, the inspiration behind Mamoo's, was a talented and passionate ice cream maker whose legacy lives on through the shop that bears his nickname. Called "Mamoo" because he couldn't say "Matthew" as a child, he tragically passed away in a motorcycle wreck at just 20 years old on April 19, 2018.

The story of Mamoo's began in early 2018, when Matthew and his brother opened Paradice Cream. Matthew handcrafted the ice cream while his brother created candies. Their collaboration was a hit, but it ended abruptly after Matthew's sudden passing, leading his brother to close the shop.

Hayden Ennis, the current owner of Mamoo's met Matthew while working at Best Buy. "It was a friendship where it felt like we'd known each other forever," Hayden recalls. Determined to honor his late friend's memory, Hayden reopened the shop on June 30, 2018, using Matthew's original recipes. To keep his legacy alive, Hayden renamed it Mamoo's, dedicating the space to the quality and creativity Matthew embodied.

One flavor, Mamoo's Gold, holds special significance. Inspired by Matthew's favorite candy, Ferrero Rocher, it was a recipe he never had the chance to serve at Paradice Cream. Discovering it in Matthew's handwritten notes while preparing to reopen, Hayden brought Mamoo's Gold to life, making it a shop staple that celebrates Matthew's innovation.

Mamoo's has 36 unique homemade flavors on rotation at all times—always with the option to be served inside of a freshly pressed and rolled waffle cone.

TRY IT YOURSELF

WHAT: Get a scoop from Mamoo's.

WHERE: The basement of the Arlington at 239 Central Ave.

COST: Ranges

PRO TIP: Looking for the perfect place to enjoy your ice cream? Take a stroll in Arlington Lawn located across the street, and visit the thermal water display spring.

Photos courtesy of Hayden Ennis

Today, Mamoo's continues to grow, balancing classic flavors Matthew created with new ideas inspired by his love of ice cream. Every scoop honors the young man whose dream endures in every bite.

THE SUNDIAL

Where is the community connection point?

At the Garland County Library, "community connection point" isn't just a slogan—it's a way of life. A shining example is their new community garden, opened on June 10, 2023.

With 42 raised beds available for checkout, the garden welcomes locals to explore their green thumbs. It also features a 17,000-square-foot pollinator haven with native plants, an orchard with apple and pear trees, muscadines, and even efforts to restore the historic Ozark chinkapin, a chestnut species nearly wiped out in the early 1900s.

But the true hidden gem of the garden is its sundial. Handmade and cast by a patron in 1955, this sundial was originally gifted to the library at its old Woodbine Street location. When the library moved, the

VISIT THE LIBRARY

WHAT: From books to movies to gardening, the library offers a multitude of activities.

WHERE: 1427 Malvern Ave.

COST: Free

PRO TIP: Anyone can become a library cardholder. If you don't live in the county, you just have to pay a small fee.

Photos courtesy of Jessamy Carter

sundial was packed away—forgotten for decades—until a worker stumbled upon it just days before the patron's great-nephew called asking about it.

This astonishing coincidence brought the sundial back into the spotlight, where it was rededicated in the perfect location: the library's community garden. It's more than a timepiece; it's a symbol of how the library preserves connections to its past while growing new traditions for the future.

Still working, the sundial is accurate within about 15 minutes of the day, depending on the time of year.

CLEANSING THERMAL WATER

Where can you bathe in the water outside?

While it's true you can safely drink the thermal spring water flowing from Hot Springs Mountain, most visitors come for the iconic experience of bathing in it. For centuries, people believed these 143-degree waters could heal sore or diseased bodies—long before modern medicine. Bathing in the spring water is a must for anyone visiting Hot Springs.

That said, many expect picturesque outdoor springs like those in Idaho, Colorado, or Oregon. Unfortunately, those don't exist here. Why? First, the springs are too hot to safely bathe in directly. At 143 degrees on average, immersion is impossible. Second, the high temperatures keep the water clean and safe to drink by killing bacteria. Allowing swimming in the pools before the water reaches public fountains would compromise its cleanliness.

This is where Hot Springs's iconic bathhouses shine, playing a pivotal role in the city's culture. For a thermal spring experience, visitors have two excellent options:

- Buckstaff Bathhouse and Quapaw Baths and Spa offer private soaking experiences in temperature-controlled tubs.
- Quapaw also features a large public pool area with various temperature-controlled pools and small waterfalls, perfect for a communal, vintage spa vibe.

Modern medicine decreased the influx of visitors coming to heal in the waters. Today, a dip in the thermal water is more of a relaxing spa treatment than a medicinal trial.

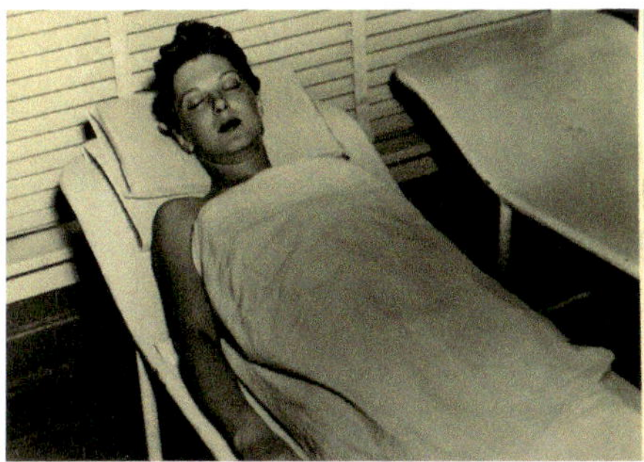

TAKE A BATH

WHAT: Soak in the thermal water pool.

WHERE: Quapaw Bathhouse

COST: Fee for admission

PRO TIP: Get there early because it is first come, first served, with no time limit on pool visitors.

Photos courtesy of Garland County Historical Society

For those determined to enjoy outdoor water activities, Hot Springs has three beautiful lakes to explore. However, for a true thermal spring experience, nothing beats the historic bathhouses, which combine relaxation with a deep connection to the city's history and culture.

ELECTRIFYING

Where did Mid-America's Tesla coil come from?

One of the most popular exhibits at Mid-America Science Museum is the Tesla Theater. This feature is thanks to locals Richard and Mary Ellen Mathias. From 2002 to 2019, this couple donated numerous Tesla coils to museums around the country, breaking Guinness World Records along the way.

Their first donation was the massive exhibit that can be found in Hot Springs's Mid-America Science Museum. Surrounded by a 2.5-ton steel cage, "Caged Lightning" is one of the museum's most popular exhibits to this day.

Each exhibit presentation features a live Tesla coil demonstration, insights into Nikola Tesla's life, and an explanation of the coil's impact on daily life. The exhibit earned the title of the world's most powerful conical coil in 2007, certified by Guinness World Records. General Electric then played a key role in partially funding all subsequent Tesla coils donated by the Mathiases to science museums, ensuring the continued awe-inspiring legacy of Tesla's creations.

The Mathiases donated two more Guinness World Record–setting Tesla coils: the most powerful bipolar musical tesla coil to Hands On! Discovery Center in 2014 and the largest bipolar musical tesla coil to the Museum of Discovery in Little Rock in 2015.

During their career, the duo created a smaller version for a traveling educational program, "Sermon from Science," which reached 22,000 students across 40 schools and organizations

---

"We've come to realize there is a time and a season for everything, and our season is over with. It's time to turn it over to the younger generation now."—Mary Ellen Mathias, the *Sentinel-Record*, 2019.

SHOCKING!

WHAT: Witness the world's most powerful Tesla coil.

WHERE: Mid-America Science Museum is located at 500 Mid America Blvd.

COST: Fee for admission

PRO TIP: Plan to spend the day at MASM—there is a lot to see.

Photos courtesty of Mid-America Science Museum

from 2003 to 2009. In 2017, the coil found a permanent home at the Tesla Science Center in Wardenclyffe, New York, on the site of Tesla's original laboratory.

Although the Mathiases have retired from making Tesla coils, the couple still makes frequent visits to their exhibit at Mid-America.

LONGHUA

Who is the world-renowned artist who calls Hot Springs home?

Hot Springs is known for its art scene, and the art scene is what called Shanghai native Longhua Xu to Hot Springs and has kept him here since 1989. As an internationally renowned artist, Xu and his late wife, Chen Shun Ying, settled in this Southern community, both creating art and raising two children.

Compared to Shanghai in the late 1980s, Xu (pronounced "shoe") said Hot Springs was quiet, peaceful, and cheap. It was also a place where he could introduce his culture through his art.

Xu's art journey started with childhood landscape painting sessions. Selected by the Chinese National Arts and Crafts Company in 1971, he mastered traditional Chinese art at Luo Qing. After graduating from East China University of Technology, he taught art until 1989. Exhibiting nationally since 1972, his works, including monumental sculptures, gained recognition.

THE VISITOR

WHAT: Xu's newest sculpture

WHERE: Hill Wheatley Plaza

COST: Free

PRO TIP: Read up on Xu's life and legacy with Arkansas Heritage, which named him the state's 2019 Living Treasure.

In 1989, Xu immigrated to the US as an "Outstanding Artist." This rare immigration class of admission allowed Xu and his family to immigrate with green cards issued exponentially faster in comparison to other immigrants. It wouldn't be long after Xu's arrival that he would begin to leave his artistic mark on Hot Springs.

In 1992, he was commissioned by the city to make *Mother Nature*, a cultured marble sculpture with a water feature that sits near the intersection in front of the Arlington Hotel.

Other of Xu's works found in the community are *Peace*, a copper sculpture located in front of the Exchange Street Parking Garage, and *Reach for the Stars*, a bronze statue at Main Street Visual & Performing Arts Magnet School. At CHI St. Vincent Hot Springs, you will find *Celebration of Life*, a bronze statue; *Healing the Sick*, a cultured marble sculpture; and more than 50 paintings by Xu hanging throughout the hospital.

Despite losing his wife in 2019, Xu continues to create new work in their downtown home studio daily and travels frequently. The studio is now connected to their two children's private medical practice, where the Xu family continues to serve and create for the community.

"The sculpture is a beautiful addition to the Bathhouse Row and should bring enjoyment to millions of visitors for years to come."—President Bill Clinton on *Mother Nature*, 1992.

Photo courtesy of Jeremy Rodgers

THIRD TIME'S THE CHARM

There were *how many* Arlingtons?

Hot Springs has been known for its numerous hotels throughout its history. The one mentioned the most is undoubtedly the Arlington, which still stands today in downtown Hot Springs. It is woven throughout stories in this book. What many may not know is that although the Arlington has been around since 1875, the structure we see today is actually the *third* Arlington.

The first Arlington started out as a large hotel on Bathhouse Row in 1872, built by former Governor Henry Rector and called Rector House. It was remodeled and enlarged in 1874, reopening as the Arlington on April 15, 1875. Built with a wood frame, it was the largest hotel in the state with 479 rooms, sitting on what is now Arlington Park.

The second Arlington was a red-brick building built to replace the wooden one in late 1892. It succumbed to Hot Springs's unfortunate history of tragic blazes on April 5, 1923.

FEAST AT THE ARLINGTON

WHAT: Friday night seafood or Sunday brunch?

WHERE: 239 Central Ave.

COST: Ranges

PRO TIP: Check out the downstairs mall where you will find ice cream, records, books, and clothing.

The third Arlington, which is the stately piece of architecture we see today, opened at 239 Central Avenue (across Fountain Street from the second Arlington) on December 31, 1924.

Over the years, the Arlington has proven to be a place of parties and luxury with famous baseball players, actresses, and even presidents coming through, as well as the infamous gangsters previously mentioned. Today (2024), a $30 million restoration is preserving the hotel's historic features.

Photos courtesy of Garland County Historical Society

"The Arlington is proud of its part in developing Hot Springs National Park as 'America's Favorite Spa.'"—Arlington President Joy Manning Scott, the *Sentinel-Record*, 1959.

YELLOWSTONE WHO?

Which came first, Hot Springs or Yellowstone?

Yellowstone National Park is widely recognized as the first national park, designated by the government on March 1, 1872. Nearly 50 years later, on March 4, 1921, Hot Springs officially added "National Park" to its name, becoming the 12th park in the system.

And let's be honest—when it comes to national park rankings, it's a bit of a beauty contest. Which landscapes left government officials so awestruck that they were crowned as America's first national treasures?

So, does it matter that Yellowstone was first and Hot Springs came in 12th? Maybe not. But in a playful *nana-nana-boo-boo* way, we like to point out that Hot Springs could have claimed the title of first. That's why we celebrate two anniversaries for the park: National Park Day in March and Reservation Day on April 20.

"For the reservation itself, one of the things that is unique is that we were among the first federally protected lands in the United States," park ranger Ashley Waymouth told the *Sentinel-Record* on April 8, 2021. "We were given the name 'reservation' because terms like 'national park' didn't exist yet."

Hot Springs National Park was originally designated a federal reservation in 1832.

"How many parks can say they've had multiple names, especially when one of those is being one of the first pieces of land to be federally owned?" Waymouth adds.

"In a lot of ways, because of our creation, we really paved the way for the National Park Service to be born."—Ashley Waymouth, the *Sentinel-Record*, 2021.

EXPLORE THE PARK

WHAT: Explore some of the trailheads in the park, which branches just off of downtown.

WHERE: Hot Springs National Park

COST: Free

PRO TIP: Go to the Lamar Bathhouse to check out a national park gift shop.

Photos courtesy of Garland County Historical Society

BOYHOOD

Which US president grew up in Hot Springs?

President Bill Clinton was born in Hope, Arkansas, as is widely acknowledged, in all likelihood because "It all began in a place called Hope" makes for a much better campaign slogan than "It all began in a place called Hot Springs." However, Clinton moved to Hot Springs when he was just 7 years old, spending his elementary through his high school years here.

BOYHOOD HOME

WHAT: See the house Clinton lived in.

WHERE: 1011 Park Ave.

COST: Free

PRO TIP: This is a private residence. Do not linger or trespass.

With the passing of Clinton's father three months before his birth, it was marriage that brought him and his mother, Virginia Cassidy Blythe, to Hot Springs in 1953. Cassidy would be married to Hot Springs car salesman Roger Clinton from 1950 to 1962, and then again after a brief divorce from 1962 until Roger's death in 1967. During the second marriage, at the age of 15, Bill officially changed his last name from Blythe to Clinton. Virginia and Roger had one son together, Roger Clinton Jr. But it wasn't always a happy homelife. Roger Clinton Sr. has often been described as a drunken gambler.

Despite an oftentimes abusive homelife with Roger, Clinton would excel academically. He actively engaged in various activities, showcasing leadership skills, a love for reading, and

---

Once a tourism attraction, Clinton's most notable boyhood home is now a private residence.

musical talent. His interest in law blossomed at Hot Springs High School, notably during a mock trial where he passionately defended the ancient Roman senator Catiline. This experience sparked his realization that he wanted to study law. Two pivotal moments in 1963 further solidified his ambition to pursue public service: his visit to the White House as a Boys Nation senator to meet President John F. Kennedy and his viewing of Martin Luther King Jr.'s iconic "I Have a Dream" speech on television, which left a lasting impression on him as he left Hot Springs and headed to Georgetown.

Photos courtesy of Garland County Historical Society

VINTAGE CLUBBING

Is Hot Springs home to Arkansas's oldest bar?

Having opened in 1905, the Ohio Club is considered Arkansas's oldest continually operating bar. With a long history of being an illegal casino that infamous gangsters liked to frequent, having a stage world-renowned acts performed on, and even at one time being a gay bar with regular drag performances in the 1970s, the modern-day establishment has done well in preserving its history through architecture and decoration. Walking into the Ohio Club looks and feels like you're in the oldest bar in the state, while retaining its high-quality classiness.

Gangsters like Al Capone, Bugsy Siegel, Bugs Moran, and Lucky Luciano enjoyed time at the Ohio Club, as did famous Major League Baseball players like Babe Ruth. Live performances by Al Jolson and Mae West have taken place on the club's stage as well.

THE OHIO CLUB

WHAT: Dine at Arkansas's oldest bar.

WHERE: 336 Central Ave.

COST: Ranges

PRO TIP: Be sure to try the locally brewed Madden beer on tap, brewed with the thermal spring waters across the street at Superior Bathhouse Brewery.

And as with anything containing that much history, there are rumors of the joint being haunted. But don't worry, haunted happenings tend to happen after hours at the Ohio Club, so don't hesitate to go on in and enjoy an old-fashioned with a burger at the bar. Or, on Thursday through Monday nights, catch a live band upstairs like the good ole days.

Don't forget to say hi to Al Capone sitting on the bench outside! He's always photo ready.

AU NATUREL

What are those locked green metal boxes in the national park?

When walking through Hot Springs National Park, you will come across locked green metal boxes. These are collection boxes where the actual thermal water springs have been capped off in order to protect them and keep them pure. Under each of the 47 spring boxes located throughout the park, there is a stainless steel cylinder connected to the spring that reroutes its water to a large reservoir beneath Bathhouse Row. There, the water is redistributed for public use through local bathhouses, display springs and fountains, and jug fountains. This system of collection boxes also allows the national park to monitor the health of the water prior to public use and consumption. More than 600,000 gallons of this water are distributed per day for public use.

ARLINGTON LAWN'S SPRING

WHAT: Visit the next best thing to a spring in its natural setting.

WHERE: 301 Crescent Ave.

COST: Free

PRO TIP: Take the staircase underneath the gazebo located to the right of the spring. This will give you even more views and take you to the Promenade where you will find some of the capped-off springs.

With the multitude of safety measures taken to protect these historic springs and keep the water available to the

---

Man-made display springs are the closest anyone can get to the thermal water in a natural setting. Here, you may only touch the water. For consumption, visit the jug fountains located throughout the park.

Photos courtesy of the National Park Service

public, many outdoor enthusiasts still want to know if there is any way to see these springs in their natural settings. I have previously mentioned why you can't bathe in the natural springs, but what about just looking at them?

Unfortunately, every spring has been capped off, and there is no way to see the original springs today. There is a man-made display spring in Arlington Lawn, and another behind the Maurice Bathhouse.

COPS VERSUS SHERIFFS

Why did two law enforcement agencies have one of the deadliest shoot-outs of their time in downtown Hot Springs?

This is a story in Hot Springs's history that accurately reflects the widely known corruption that ran the town during the 20th century. What started as a political war over money and power ended in a deadly shoot-out in the streets on March 16, 1899.

I don't know what's more shocking: the fact this shoot-out's fatalities triumphed over the infamous gunfight at the O.K. Corral, the fact it was between two law enforcement agencies, or the fact no one was ever held accountable for the deaths of five men.

It began when one mayoral candidate pledged ongoing tenure to Hot Springs Police Chief Thomas C. Toler, while another assured Garland County Sheriff R. L. "Bob" Williams a continued role and also offered his brother a position as chief of police. But there was a little bit more at stake than just a title.

In 1899, gambling was illegal yet a very lucrative business in Hot Springs, so everyone wanted control of it. Having hands in both city and county law enforcement would be ideal for the Williams brothers. As the political race heated up, so did the tension between the once-friendly Toler and Williams.

WELCOME TO THE WILD WEST

WHAT: Play dress up like you're in the Wild West.

WHERE: Tombstone Old Time Photo up the street at 320 Central Ave.

COST: Varies upon guests.

PRO TIP: Dive deeper into Hot Springs' history after leaving the shop, and have your pick between the Wax Museum or Gangster museum — both just a few doors down.

Photo courtesy of Garland County Historical Society

When Williams caught word on March 16, 1899, of a political caucus held by Toler with his department and favored candidate, weapons were drawn between Williams, his son, and an HSPD deputy. No one was hurt, and later in the day, Toler and his deputy arranged for an in-person meeting with the Williamses in an effort to make amends.

Upon arriving at a saloon on Central Avenue just north of its intersection with Bridge Street, an HSPD captain accused a sheriff's deputy of threatening him. The captain's brother-in-law, the saloon's bartender, intervened, slashing the deputy's neck. Injured, the deputy fired shots at the bartender, initiating the shoot-out with members from both agencies involved.

Toler, Williams's son, the bartender, and an HSPD sergeant all died. Williams, who showed up moments after the shoot-out, fatally shot one more member of the HSPD who had also just arrived on the scene.

Williams and three others in his department were charged with unjustifiable homicide but were all found not guilty. Williams went on to serve a total of nine terms as sheriff.

BOOM GOES THE DYNAMITE

Why was Hot Springs blowing up in the 1960s?

Shoot-outs aren't the only act of violence surrounding gambling in Hot Springs's history. After decades of widespread illegal gambling, the townspeople's favorite vice saw an explosive few years. From 1963 to 1968, there was a series of six bombings. The cases that left none dead were never solved, although the same type of dynamite was used in each instance. The town has nothing but theories half a century later.

"Indeed, it has been suggested that the gambling interests of the 1950s and 1960s realized that the more they ran legitimate and noncontroversial gambling operations, the less scrutiny they would receive from state and federal authorities," historian Clay Farrar said in a September 26, 2018, *Sentinel-Record* article.

Despite this more peaceful coexistence, the mysterious series of bombings began on January 4, 1963, at the Vapors Casino.

"The explosion took place in the morning while staff training was underway," Farrar said. "Eleven employees were injured. . . . The casino was put out of operation for several weeks just as its peak spring season was about to begin."

On April 23, 1963, prosecuting attorney David Whittington's vehicle was blown up around midnight. A bombing attempt was made at the home of Velda Rose Tower Motor Hotel manager Gerald Vanderslice, but the two sticks

---

"There is a good chance that even today someone in the Hot Springs community has knowledge about who committed these crimes."—Clay Farrar, the *Sentinel-Record*, 2018.

of dynamite thrown in his yard failed to explode.

On March 30, 1966, four cars at Vapors Casino owner Dane Harris's private residence were struck with dynamite. Later that night, dynamite exploded at the private residence of Circuit Judge P. E. Dobbs, damaging his vehicle.

On February 12, 1968, Raymond Clinton (President Bill Clinton's uncle), was the final bombing target when his vehicle was damaged by explosives at his lake house.

VAPORS LIVE

WHAT: Visit the site of one of the biggest bombings, which now operates as a live show venue.

WHERE: 315 Park Ave.

COST: Ranges

PRO TIP: Author David Hill's grandmother worked at the Vapors at the time of the bombings. Hill documented her story in his highly praised true crime book, *The Vapors*.

Photo courtesy of Garland County Historical Society

DONS

Where is the speakeasy?

Located in the heart of historic downtown Hot Springs, DONS Southern Social is a speakeasy that provides a unique twist on Southern favorites in a setting perfect for friends and fellowship. This spot operates differently from typical restaurants, adding an element of intrigue to the dining experience.

To start your adventure at DONS, you'll need a reservation. After booking, you'll receive an email and text with details on how to find the entrance and the secret password required for entry. True to speakeasy tradition, DONS keeps things discreet. Reservations are strongly recommended to secure your spot in this exclusive experience.

When your GPS indicates you've arrived at DONS, you might be puzzled by the lack of visible signage. However, the clue provided with your reservation will guide you to the entrance. One entrance is cleverly concealed behind a bookcase that swings open. The decor inside blends industrial and cozy

DONS SOUTHERN SOCIAL

WHAT: Downtown's speakeasy

WHERE: 901 Central Ave.

COST: $$$

PRO TIP: Check out the owner's other restaurant, the Best Cafe, for brunch!

Hot Springs, once a hot spot for gangsters like Al Capone during Prohibition, is the perfect town for a speakeasy-themed restaurant. Back then, secret speakeasies were part of the local nightlife.

Top left, bottom left, bottom right: *Photos courtesy of Bailey Anne Studios*
Top right: *Photo courtesy of Visit Hot Springs*

elements with exposed brick, a wood-plank ceiling, and a warm wooden bar area.

A notable feature at DONS is the kitchen window near the bar, where you can watch the chefs in action. Owned by chef Joshua Garland, a Little Rock native who also owns Best Cafe and Bar in Hot Springs, DONS is a culinary delight. The menu features innovative takes on Southern classics, ensuring every dish is a pleasant surprise. DONS Southern Social offers a dining experience that is both unique and memorable, making it a must-visit spot in Hot Springs.

FREEDOM

What happened to *Freedom*?

Today, at the intersection of Central Avenue and Market Street, you will see a black wall with windows. Prior to February 15, 2023, it was a colorful portrait depicting abolitionist Harriet Tubman leading the way to freedom.

The *Freedom* mural was completed by Little Rock–based artist Perrion Hurd in a collaboration with local kids on November 21, 2021. Underneath Tubman were individually painted people walking with her. These figures were painted by local students.

When DONS Southern Social, a Black-owned business, moved into the building with the intention of opening its speakeasy, the mural was covered up to play into the restaurant's desire to be discreet. DONS is a favorite, not only locally but across the state. Despite this, its success came at a cost for Hurd's mural.

"The basic premise of the mural is, in my opinion, we all get to freedom together," Hurd told the *Hot Springs Post* in 2021. "And I hope that by me doing this mural in the community of Hot Springs—right across the street from where there is a Confederate statue—I hope it gives people an opportunity to talk."

Hurd's mural was located directly across the street from a Confederate monument that stands tall in Como Triangle. To make matters worse, the area has a dark history attached to it, as discussed in the following section.

Commissioned by the Hot Springs Area Cultural Alliance, a nonprofit, the *Freedom* mural was displayed for less than two years before being covered.

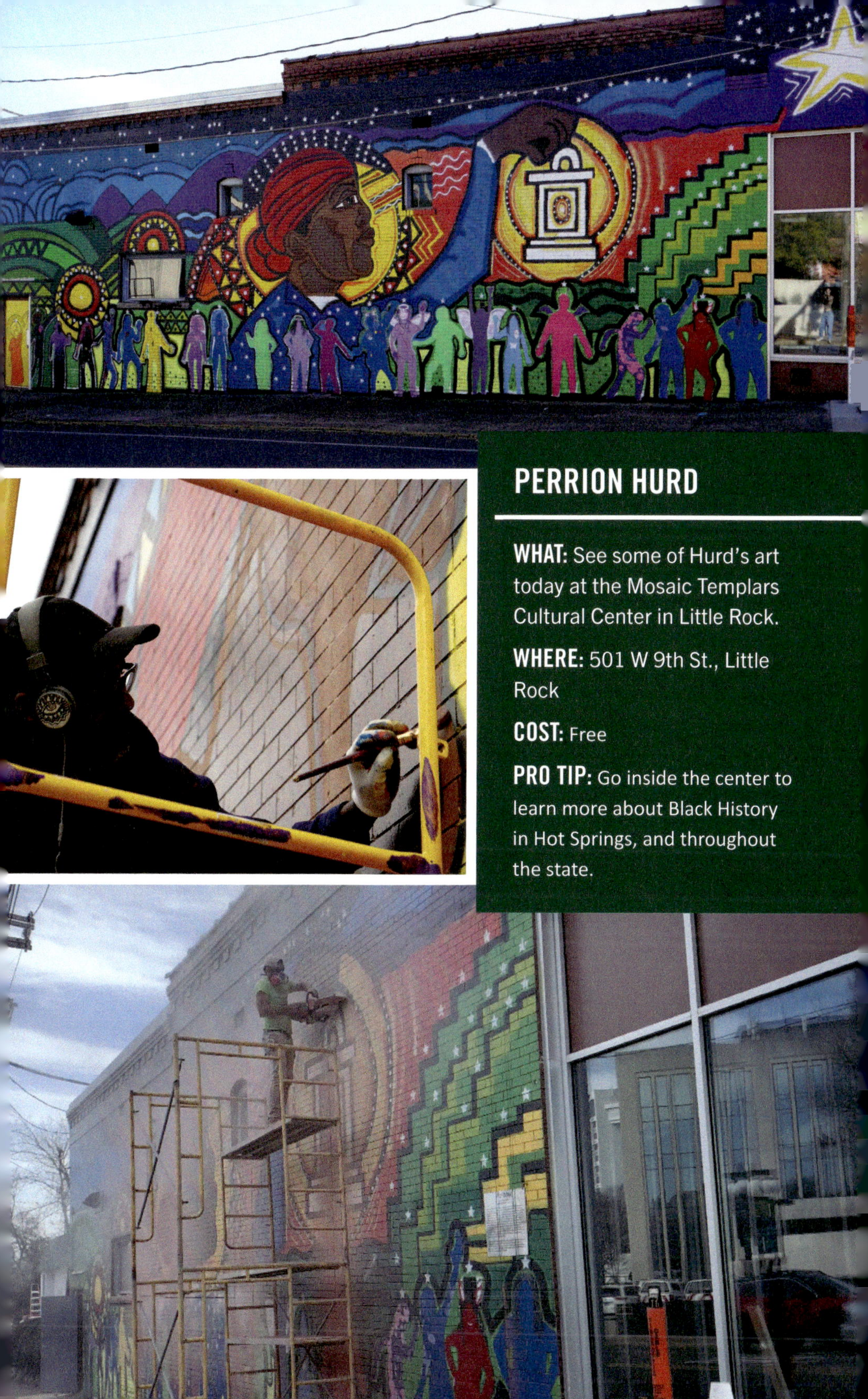

PERRION HURD

WHAT: See some of Hurd's art today at the Mosaic Templars Cultural Center in Little Rock.

WHERE: 501 W 9th St., Little Rock

COST: Free

PRO TIP: Go inside the center to learn more about Black History in Hot Springs, and throughout the state.

GILBERT HARRIS

What happened at Como Square and who was Gilbert Harris?

Before the Como area was a privately owned triangle containing a Confederate monument in downtown Hot Springs, it was a public square with a light pole. As the area at the intersection of Central and Ouachita Avenues was restructured over the years, Como Square became Como Triangle, and the city gifted the land to the United Daughters of the Confederacy. A Confederate monument was erected at the location in 1934 by the UDC.

Surrounding this area is a shameful history Hot Springs shies away from. It's best told by late local historian Orval Allbritton in his book *Leo and Verne*.

The tragic incident unfolded after the untimely 1922 death of Maurice Connelly, a young, well-known White man employed at the Arkansas Bank and Trust Company. Returning home from a rooftop dance to his Orange Street apartment, he encountered an armed burglar, resulting in a struggle in which Connelly was shot and fatally wounded. The assailant, identified as a Black man named Gilbert Harris, fled into the night, sparking a citywide manhunt.

Police Chief Sullivan, accompanied by Constable Bert Hall, tracked Harris to his home. Despite Harris's arrest, a mob gathered outside the City Hall building, in which the jail was located, demanding swift justice. Mayor Harry A. Jones and former Circuit Judge Scott Wood attempted to reason with the crowd, but the situation escalated.

CONFEDERATE MONUMENT

WHAT: The site of two lynchings marked with a Confederate monument

WHERE: The intersections of Central, Market, and Ouachita

COST: Free

PRO TIP: The park centrally located in downtown Hot Springs is considered private property, with a "no trespassing" sign posted.

Mayor Jones, standing before Harris's cell, pleaded for restraint but was ignored. The mob dragged Harris into the streets, placed him in a truck, and headed to Como Square.

In a horrifying display on August 1, 1922, the mob lynched Harris, pulling a rope up the telephone pole until he strangled to death. The police intervened after 15 minutes, taking possession of the lifeless body.

An inquest deemed Harris's death to have come at the hands of the mob, witnessed by hundreds, but the verdict served little purpose. No charges were brought against any members of the mob. The community, shocked and subdued, faced embarrassment as the lynching was reluctantly acknowledged. An editorial in the *Sentinel-Record* attempted to justify the act, claiming it would curb house robberies and asserting there was no racial prejudice involved. No information on Harris's life outside of his murder was uncovered during the research of this book.

This was the second of two lynchings at the Como site in Hot Springs's history. The first was of a man named Will Norman in 1913.

The lynching of Harris, a painful chapter said to have been rarely discussed in polite conversation for many years, cast a dark shadow over Hot Springs.

WAXY HORRORS

What's behind the bypass door on the wax museum tour?

Let's be honest, wax museums are often unintentionally creepy. There is no exception for the Josephine Tussaud Wax Museum. As you walk up the staircase to enter the museum, some of the first wax figures you see are Presidents Barack Obama and Jimmy Carter, and Steve McQueen on a motorcycle. (Try not to look too hard or you will be convinced their eyes are following you.) At the top of the staircase there is a suspended cross with a dying Jesus covered in bottom dressings hanging from it. Behind him is a re-creation of Leonardo da Vinci's *The Last Supper*. This is just the start of the wax museum tour, and we haven't even gotten to the part that's "not recommended for small children."

TOUR THE MUSEUM

WHAT: Can you brave the wax museum?

WHERE: 250 Central Ave.

COST: Fee for admission

PRO TIP: Be sure to check out the museum's 4D virtual reality feature.

Hang a left at *The Last Supper*, and you will be greeted by Alfred Hitchcock. This is the part where you can decide if you want to pursue the intended horrors behind the curtain to your left or take a right and continue on your merry way.

As someone who has an affinity for haunted houses and all things spooky, I can honestly say the horror part of this tour is bone-chilling. There are no jump scares or blind spots, but there are real-life depictions of brutal ancient execution methods like torture by ants and pendulum, representations of the 1642 Irish massacre where 40,000 Protestants were sacrificed, and a few fictional horrors like Frankenstein's monster, a werewolf, a vampire, and a zombie for good measure.

The realism behind this horror exhibit is jarring, and not what comes to anyone's mind when desiring to visit downtown Hot Springs's wax museum.

The horrors continue throughout the tour with scenes such as Abraham Lincoln's assassination and Teddy Roosevelt on horseback, both recognized as haunted hot spots by paranormal investigators.

SKYSCRAPER OF HEALTH AND HEROES

Was the Medical Arts Building the inspiration behind the *Daily Planet* building?

It's widely rumored the tall, art deco Medical Arts Building in downtown Hot Springs was used in the 1950s TV series *Adventures of Superman* starring George Reeves. Some rumors even say scenes of the show were filmed here. *Forbes* magazine even claims the image of the building was used in early Superman movies.

One story, as recounted by blogger Dayton Ward in 2019, is that the first illustrator of the Superman comic was on vacation in Hot Springs, staying at the Arlington Hotel, which sits across the street from the Medical Arts Building. He saw the building in all its beauty, and as a result, the *Daily Planet's* building made its debut in the comics in 1940.

But is this truth or tale? Let's start with some facts about the Medical Arts Building that still stands tall after nearly a century.

This 16-story building was built in 1930. It was the tallest building in the state and Arkansas's first skyscraper, housing dozens of physician offices.

In 1978, the building was placed on the National Register of Historic Places but was steadily vacated over the following decade with the last physician leaving in 1991.

The Medical Arts Building was sold in pieces over the years, and by 2021 it had four owners over different sections until local hotelier Parth Patel purchased all but the 16th floor with plans to renovate the building into a hotel. At the time of this book's publishing, the building is still under renovation by Patel.

While I cannot prove or disprove any *Superman* illustrator spent some time with us, I can confirm that Superman's cocreator Joe Shuster worked as a newsboy at the *Toronto Star*, and Shuster has apparently made claims that that art

LOOK, UP IN THE SKY!

WHAT: Learn about this lore and all things superhero at The Galaxy Connection Museum.

WHERE: 536 Ouachita Ave.

COST: Fee for admission

PRO TIP: See the building for yourself at 236 Central Ave. Want a better view? Head across the street to Arlington Park. Take the staircase at the gazebo up until you reach the Promenade. Take a right and you will see a viewing area.

deco building (which has characteristics similar to the Medical Arts Building) is what inspired the *Daily Planet* building.

The silver lining? Now that the *Toronto Star* building has been demolished, perhaps the Medical Arts is the best you can get for an in-person feel of the *Daily Planet* in real life.

Regardless of Superman lore, the Medical Arts Building remains a cherished historic landmark, with its independent restoration eagerly anticipated.

CAT NEVER SAW THE BAG

How did Hot Springs run illegal gambling operations publicly?

From 1927 to 1967, illegal gambling (along with thermal bathing until its decline in the mid-1940s) was what kept Hot Springs running, and this wasn't a little-known fact. You may be wondering, *How did Hot Springs illegally gamble so . . . publicly?* In short, the answer is money. In the 2018 Garland County Historical Society *Record*, Clay Farrar outlines the nationwide coverage Hot Springs's reputation had.

"The state of Arkansas has disowned Hot Springs. It's a municipal harlot, not fit to associate with the Bible-minded members of the family," a January 23, 1946, article in the *New York World-Telegram* reads.

But if everyone knew, how did it go on for so long? We could sum it up to "different times," but dirty politicians and paid-off police officers are a more accurate point of the finger.

"Hell, we violate the law down here every day in the year except Sundays," Hot Springs Mayor Leo P. McLaughlin was reported saying in the *New York World-Telegram*.

Also, most people simply did not care. Garland County Historical Society Executive Director Liz Robbins notes there was always a portion of the population opposed to the illegal gambling—especially ministers and church groups.

"Of course this town's illegal, but it's been running open for years. People expect it and want it," casino owner Dane Harris said in a March 19, 1962, *Sports Illustrated* article.

The key to the clubs being able to operate openly had always been their relationships with local politicians.

"Politicians tolerated the gambling because it brought growth to the city, additional tax revenue, and money for them," Wayne Threadgill said in his book *Gambling in the Spa*.

Gambling was shut down for good when Arkansas Governor Winthrop Rockefeller was elected in 1967. Hot Springs felt the economic sting in the years to come. Today, one of the largest tourism draws is legally boasting about these past illegal happenings.

"The Mob did not run the gambling operation in Hot Springs. The local people did. That is the most common misconception about the illegal gambling era."—Liz Robbins, Garland County Historical Society executive director, 2024.

LOCAL GAMBLING

WHAT: Where can you gamble today?

WHERE: 2705 Central Ave.

COST: Hopefully less than you win

PRO TIP: There is only one local casino in operation today (and yes, it's totally legal). Come test your luck at Oaklawn Racing Casino Resort!

Photos courtesy of Garland County Historical Society

LIGHTS, CAMERA, ACTION

What's behind the scenes of the local film scene?

A lot of things come to mind when you think of Hot Springs. Hiking, bathhouses, and gambling, to name a few. It's an eclectic bunch that make up the landscape, and many of these microcommunities are mentioned throughout this book. One growing community in Hot Springs is a surprising one: the film community. Filmmaking is likely not the first thing that comes to mind when you think of Hot Springs, or even Arkansas. Yet it's quickly becoming a force to be reckoned with through film festivals and filmmaking programs.

Thanks to the local nonprofit Low Key Arts, the return home of filmmaker and Hot Springs native Jen Gerber, who has overseen every local film program in some capacity—and the efforts of a slew of other driven volunteers—has led to tremendous growth of the filmmaking and film-loving community. It all started with the inception of the Hot Springs Documentary Film Festival in 1991. Now, after more than three decades, this nine-day festival is North America's longest-running documentary film festival. Another festival to note is the Arkansas Shorts film festival, which has recently been rebranded as Low Key Arts's Persistence of Vision Film Festival (POV Fest).

"Whether making a film is on your bucket list or a desired career path, I2P [Inception to Projection] provides opportunities for filmmakers of all levels to create and showcase original work."—Low Key Arts.

CATCH A FILM

WHAT: POV Fest (formerly known as Arkansas Shorts) is held every January.

WHERE: Downtown Hot Springs

COST: Ranges

PRO TIP: Look for the films with the Inception to Projection logo in the opening. This will indicate which films have been created locally.

Photos courtesy of Jen Gerber

In addition to showcasing films, great lengths have been taken to assist aspiring filmmakers through programs like Inception to Projection, which helps to bring their visions to life on the same stages as filmmakers around the world.

CHEESE CREDIT

Was cheese dip created in Hot Springs?

Arkansas takes cheese dip very seriously—it has fought for the title of creator with Texas since the ooey gooey, warm, and inviting side dish was introduced to southern communities in the early 1900s. (That's right, the delicious Mexican restaurant staple did indeed originate in the southern US rather than Latin America.) Assuming Arkansas did create cheese dip first, what many people don't know is that there is an internal battle about where in Arkansas cheese dip was created. Was it in Hot Springs or an hour up the road in Little Rock?

With Little Rock holding the annual World Cheese Dip Championship, it's widely assumed Little Rock is where cheese dip originated. That and the fact that Mexico Chiquito, the place that claims to have invented the dip, is in Little Rock still today.

Due to scarce records, here's what we think we know, and what puts the creation of cheese dip most likely in Hot Springs:

Cheese dip was created by a man named Blackie Donnelly and his wife in 1935, when the pair moved to Hot Springs from Texas. They owned and operated a restaurant called Little Mexico in Hot Springs, which is where it's thought the dip was introduced. Within an estimated decade, the two moved their business to North Little Rock and renamed it Mexico Chiquito.

Today, Texas claims queso and Arkansas claims cheese dip—but is there really a difference? Either way, both states can enjoy their titles, letting Texas's annual Quesoff and Arkansas's Cheese Dip Championship coexist peacefully.

OUR CHEESE DIP

WHAT: Where to get the cheese

WHERE: This is the south—throw a rock in any direction and you're sure to hit a good Mexican restaurant.

COST: A large bowl of cheese dip ranges from $7–$13

PRO TIP: Curious about the documentary that sparked the debate over the origin of cheese dip in Arkansas? Check out Nick Rogers's very 2000s documentary, *A Movie About Cheese Dip*, on Vimeo.

But does it really matter which borders held a kitchen one fateful moment when perhaps one of the Donnellys had the bright idea to melt a pile of extra cheese lying around, throw some spices in, and dunk a chip in it? To some, very much so. But to most, we're just glad to have it available on the table of nearly every restaurant in the area. And it's a pretty hard dish to mess up.

Some of the best local cheese dips can be found at Picante's Mexican Grill, La Hacienda Mexican Restaurant, and Colorado Grill.

GIZMOE

Who is Hot Springs's clown?

If every town doesn't have a clown, every town should. Luckily for Hot Springs, we have Gizmoe gracing our downtown streets. Working for tips and smiles, Gizmoe can be found most Saturdays in front of Ginger's Popcorn handing out balloon art and laughs. This street clown can do it all, entertaining passersby with music and silly banter.

A Sheridan native, this clown is no novice. Gizmoe has been clowning in some capacity for 35 years. He moved to Hot Springs in 2009 and notes he wishes he had done it 20 years earlier. Not everywhere is as clown-friendly of a place as Hot Springs, Gizmoe says.

When you come across Gizmoe, he may sing you Elvis or some hit from the 1970s or '80s. There may be a conversation held with his puppet parrot. You may also be gifted a balloon flower, sword, or animal at random.

Gizmoe can be found in other areas of Hot Springs, too. When not in the daylight of downtown, he may be found performing as Gilroy the Jester at the Hot Springs Renaissance Faire, as Spanky Bottoms at local burlesque shows, or as the Joker at comic cons. And sometimes, he may not be a clown at all, but instead perhaps a superhero, Santa Claus, or the Easter Bunny. When dressed as the average man on the weekdays, he sells furniture. This clown is a jack-of-all-trades.

MEET GIZMOE

WHAT: Find Gizmoe the clown

WHERE: Downtown Hot Springs

COST: Tips and smiles

PRO TIP: Gizmoe can usually be found around Ginger's Popcorn or Rolando's on Saturdays.

"I don't believe you can fight the darkness, but I believe you can make the world a little better by being a source of light."—Gizmoe, 2024.

PRESERVING HISTORY

Does Hot Springs have the largest African American historic district in Arkansas?

The beautiful and historic John Lee Webb House sits in the Pleasant Street Historic District of Hot Springs awaiting restoration with a team of people trying to make that happen. It's a symbol of a district that represents a large portion of the city's historic African American community—including a number of homes lacking restoration left to be forgotten by anyone who doesn't call the district home. Which is especially unfortunate since this is the largest African American historic district in Arkansas.

RESTORING THE WEBB HOUSE

WHAT: A Black history preservation project under P.H.O.E.B.E.

WHERE: 403 Pleasant St.

COST: Donations may be made at theuzuriproject.org.

PRO TIP: The restoration of the house also supports the Uzuri Project, which works to preserve all facets of local Black history.

"Luckily, people passionate about the district's history have been addressing this problem in recent years," Garland County Historical Society Executive Director Liz Robbins says. "The city of Hot Springs's Malvern Avenue Gateway Corridor Improvement Project has led to many visible improvements, and the Gateway Community Association is also greatly involved in preserving the rich heritage of the Pleasant Street Historic District.

"And the Webb House? It was acquired in 2014 by the nonprofit P.H.O.E.B.E. (People Helping Others Excel by Example), led by Cheryl Batts. They are working hard to preserve this symbol of African American history."

John Lee Webb, born in 1877 in Tuskegee, Alabama, began his journey at 19 when he enlisted in the US Army during the Spanish–American War. Afterward, he pursued

a career as a general contractor in Arkansas and Mississippi.

"Webb brought the national headquarters of the Woodmen of Union fraternity to Hot Springs in 1918," Robbins says. "He built the Woodmen of Union (later the National Baptist Hotel and now Harbor Home) building at 501 Malvern Avenue in 1923–24. It became the hub of Black social, medical, and business life. It contained a 100-bed hospital, a nurses training school, a 75-room hotel, a thermal bathhouse, a bank, a 2,500-seat auditorium, a printing plant, and offices for Black professionals."

Robbins goes on to say that besides being a builder, architect, and businessman, Webb was a philanthropist. He donated the Emma Elease Webb Community Center building to the Black community of Garland County in 1945. The center to this day provides educational, social, and creative programs to the Black community.

The historic significance of Webb's legacy is embodied in the house he once called home. Situated in the heart of the Pleasant Street Historic District, the residence, initially constructed around 1900 in the frame Victorian style, underwent significant enhancements by Webb himself in the 1920s, including the addition of a brick veneer and a distinctive green-tile roof. The iconic dark-red brick, synonymous with Webb's architectural contributions to the neighborhood, adorns not only his former residence but also notable structures like Home Harbor on Malvern Avenue.

Webb wielded significant influence within the local African American community, earning recognition as one of Hot Springs's foremost citizens upon his passing in 1946.

HAPPY HOLLOW

What happened at Happy Hollow?

Happy Hollow amusement park was one of the most popular tourist destinations in Hot Springs, attracting regular visits from Al Capone when he came to town, as well as many of the Major League Baseball players who came for spring training. The amusement park was a place where "tycoons and millionaires rubbed elbows," Jessie Gnat Terry wrote in the Garland County Historical Society's 1981 *Record*.

"To 'get there,' follow the 'gang,'" was the all-too-accurate verbiage printed in a 1903 city directory ad promoting Happy Hollow amusement park. This was an attraction that brought droves of people to downtown's Fountain Street from the late 1880s to 1948.

This quirky park was started by local photographer Norman McLeod as a picture studio before he developed it into McLeod's Amusement Park and then eventually Happy Hollow amusement park. It was located at 315 Fountain Street.

People could be photographed as cowboys, clowns, Native Americans, and fat men or women in front of backdrops of hillbilly shacks, bars, or other rustic scenes. One of the most popular photo scenes was posing in a bathtub—something men would often do shirtless to appear nude. Photos were "taken in any position and under any circumstances," as read on a Happy Hollow ad. The photos made for great souvenirs.

"Those donkeys cute . . . will thrill you with delight . . . The music, songs, and dancing will soon set you right."—Norman McLeod, original song printed on visitor souvenirs.

...lk corniness flourishes mightily at Hot Springs, where two outdoor studios manage to keep busy ...aphing visiting bathers in quaint poses for having-wonderful-time-wish-you-were-here post cards.

Photo courtesy of Garland County Historical Society

THE LAST PIECE OF HAPPY HOLLOW LEFT

WHAT: Drink from the cold-water Happy Hollow Spring.

WHERE: Fountain St.

COST: Free

PRO TIP: Bring a jug to take some of this fresh spring water along with you.

"Historian Tom Dillard believes the hundreds of thousands of Happy Hollow 'hillbilly' photos sent across the country as postcards were greatly responsible for Arkansas acquiring a hillbilly image," Garland County Historical Society Executive Director Liz Robbins says.

Another popular attraction was the 100 or more caged wild animals; burros, ponies, and horses could be rented for rides up Hot Springs Mountain. A large black bear wrestled a man in a daily entertainment that often ended in injuries when the bear slapped the man too hard.

"Finally the bear became too old to fight and mysteriously disappeared," Terry writes. "In a few days on display in one of the butcher shop windows was a dressed bear hanging by its forefeet and there was a sign 'Bear Meat For Sale.' An investigation took place, and the owner of the bear said he butchered the bear and sold it to the meat market. The sign came down and there was no bear meat sold."

McLeod was quite the philanthropist, renting his cottages to people in need (often not collecting rent) and helping the sick who came to Hot Springs for thermal water treatment. He sold his interest in Happy Hollow in 1908 to Dave Anselberg. The park continued operation until Anselberg's death in 1948.

BASEMENT JAMS

What's that noise coming from the bottom of the Arlington?

The Arlington Resort Hotel & Spa is a regal piece of history that sits just below Hot Springs Mountain in downtown Hot Springs. As it was intended to, this hotel exudes grandeur, luxury, and elegance. It's an experience just to visit, regardless of whether or not you're checking in. Tourists will come through the lobby, perhaps to enjoy a live band on a Friday night or to view the glass-encased historical archives. But there is one thing in the Arlington that tourists may not expect to find: a funky retro record emporium in its basement. You may even be able to hear it from the street or lobby.

At first glance, Downtown Record & CD Emporium is an odd fit for somewhere like the Arlington. But after thumbing through Thomas Coleman's extensive vinyl collection that ranges from Edison Records to Beyoncé, you will see the two fit well together in their appreciation and preservation of history. The contrast in historical experiences just looks a little different. For example, on the first floor of the Arlington you may find a traditional fine dining or Victorian bathhouse experience, while in the basement you may find the first pressing of Metallica's *Master of Puppets* or one of the last copies of Pink Floyd's *The Wall* signed by both Roger Waters *and* David Gilmour. It's really a toss-up, but there is no shortage of treasures to be uncovered while visiting the Arlington.

Coleman, who has been in the business since 1981, says he hopes he stays the Arlington's "best kept secret." When curious explorers happen upon the shop rather than seek it out, it's recognized for the treasure it is.

DOWNTOWN RECORD & CD EMPORIUM

WHAT: Shop the Record Emporium.

WHERE: 239 Central Ave. in the Arlington's basement

COST: Ranges

PRO TIP: Be sure to visit Coleman's neighbors in the basement: Black Ribbon Books and Mamoo's Creamery.

RESILIENCE

How has downtown Hot Springs survived natural disaster after natural disaster?

The Majestic fire (later mentioned in this book) was not unique to downtown Hot Springs. This town has suffered a tremendous number of other fires and natural disasters in its history—from fire to flood to landslide. According to Isabel Anthony's *Garland County, Arkansas: Our History and Heritage*, these disasters wreaked havoc on the local economy. Three major fires in 1878, 1905, and 1913 destroyed much of the city's business and residential districts, and in 1923, 1956, and 1990, major floods severely damaged downtown stores. It's almost as if the town attracts absurd disasters.

But if Hot Springians are anything, they're resilient. And while disasters did create hits to the economy, there is a silver lining in some cases because these disasters drew people here, as the curiosity surrounding catastrophe often does.

On May 21, 1990, as Hot Springs was recovering from a massive flood a few days prior, Melinda Gassaway with the *Sentinel-Record* perfectly

BURIED CARS OF HOT SPRINGS

WHAT: A unique bit of Hot Springs history lies hidden beneath the parking lot next to The Arlington Hotel: 13 cars buried by a 1984 landslide. The massive rockslide not only covered the cars but also reshaped the parking area and added stability to the hillside.

WHERE: The parking lot beside The Arlington Hotel, heading up Central Avenue in downtown Hot Springs. Look for the rocky slope that marks the landslide's footprint.

COST: Free to visit! It's an open parking area and public space.

PRO TIP: Keep an eye out for the rocky area of Hot Springs Mountain — it's not just a natural feature, but a reminder of nature's power and the stories buried beneath the surface. Great for history buffs and curious visitors.

Photos courtesy of Garland County Historical Society

encapsulated the reaction of passersby and sense of community amid disaster in an article titled "Disaster Brings Out People's Best, Worst."

"But, while curious onlookers clogged the city's main thoroughfare, hampering cleanup efforts, [hampering] owners, and pushing and shoving their way down the sidewalks to gawk at sodden merchandise and piles of debris, anxious property owners and an army of volunteers showed the gritty spirit of this resort/retirement community."

Disaster after disaster, the Hot Springs community has made a big comeback possible each time.

DRYDEN

What's Dryden Pottery's pivotal role in the local art scene?

Founded by Alan Dryden in 1946, Dryden Pottery initially operated in Ellsworth, Kansas, providing utilitarian ware in a postwar era marked by scarcity.

After 10 years, the business relocated to Hot Springs due to declining highway traffic in Ellsworth, capitalizing on Hot Springs's status as a resort hub. Recognizing the local lack of an artistic presence, Dryden innovated by offering free factory tours, becoming a local attraction. Over the years, the pottery became a cornerstone of the Hot Springs community, influencing other artists to settle here.

With three generations now involved, Dryden Pottery continues to thrive, driven by a passion for craftsmanship and the joy it brings to collectors. Despite financial success, the family emphasizes their dedication to the art form, considering their work a labor of love rather than solely a profit-driven venture.

The Dryden family is a fixture in Hot Springs's artistic legacy, and their pieces are found around the world thanks to visitors who take these precious pieces of Hot Springs back home with them. You never know where you might find a unique piece of Dryden pottery. You can always spot one by looking at the bottom to see "Dryden" carved into the clay.

HEAD TO DRYDEN

WHAT: Buy some pottery of your own.

WHERE: 341 Whittington Ave.

COST: Ranges

PRO TIP: Request a personalized name mug to make your treasure that much more special!

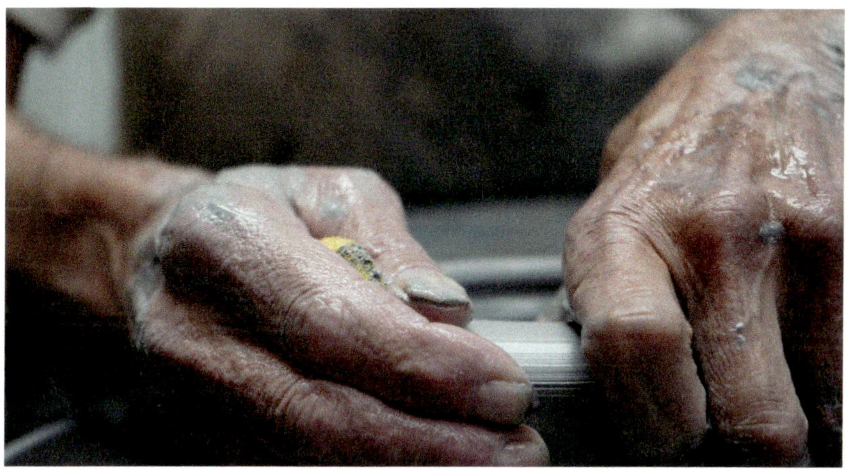

"My success comes from a labor of love. We don't really do it to make a lot of money, but we do it because it's an enjoyable life and I'm living the American artist's dream, I suppose."—Zack Dryden, the *Sentinel-Record*, 2021.

A COURTSHIP

Who was the gangster who called Hot Springs home?

In 1903, 12-year-old Owney "The Killer" Madden emigrated from England and joined the tough Gophers Gang in New York City's Hell's Kitchen. He killed his first man by the age of 17. By the time he was 23, he was suspected of shooting five men to death.

In 1915, he went to prison for the killing of a Gopher rival, William "Little Patsy Doyle" Moore. He served nine years of his 10-year sentence, then worked his way up to the top of a Prohibition bootlegging empire that brought in millions each year.

In 1931, it was a vacation that brought Madden to Hot Springs, and a local shopkeeper and postmaster's daughter, Agnes Demby, who kept him here. The two met while he was visiting, and they spent two weeks together.

Before Madden returned to New York, he gave Demby money for a train ticket to come see him. She did, but Madden's return to New York was complicated due to legalities involving his parole for the killing of Moore. Eventually, Madden went back to prison to complete the rest of his 10-year sentence.

THROUGH CRIME AND IN HEALTH

WHAT: The final resting place of Owney Madden, a notorious Prohibition-era gangster and Hot Springs nightclub owner, and his wife, Agnes Demby.

WHERE: Greenwood Cemetery, 701 Greenwood Ave., Hot Springs, Arkansas. Look for the headstones bearing their names near the entrance.

COST: Free to visit, but donations to the cemetery are always appreciated to help with upkeep.

PRO TIP: Bring a camera or notepad to document the visit — it's a great stop for history lovers or fans of true crime lore. While there, take a moment to explore other historic graves in Greenwood Cemetery, some dating back to the 19th century!

Photo courtesy of Garland County Historical Society

After just seven months, Madden was released early from his sentence once again. At his parole hearing, Madden told the board he wanted to move to Hot Springs and marry the postmaster's daughter. This time, the conditions of his parole would move with him to Hot Springs, and he would not be allowed to leave Arkansas for the remainder of his parole.

Madden turned over his New York rackets to Lucky Luciano and Frank Costello and headed back to Hot Springs. He and Agnes were married in the Demby home at 506 West Grand Avenue in 1935.

"They lived there for the rest of their lives. Madden entertained vacationing underworld figures but also made friends locally," Garland County Historical Society Executive Director Liz Robbins says. "He boated on Lake Hamilton in a Chris-Craft boat given to him by [actor] George Raft, who delighted locals by signing autographs.

"Madden spent afternoons in the Southern Club Grill, picking up the checks for soldiers and giving money to those down on their luck. Madden also gave generously to local charities."

Hot Springs loved Owney Madden.

"When Owney Madden got off the bus to become a citizen of Hot Springs, he became a truly different man and real citizen," State Senator Q. Byrum Hurst said at Madden's funeral in 1965. "For 30 years he has given his all to Hot Springs, trying to make it a better place in which to live and raise children."

"When Owney Madden arrived in the Spa City, he had been arrested 57 times and convicted twice."—Orval Allbritton, *The Mob at the Spa.*

MOUNTAIN MOVER

What's the best way to trek both mountains in one morning?

Hot Springs caters to many different communities, as mentioned throughout this book. There is something for everyone, including those in the sizable running community. From local groups like the Spa City Pacers to visitors from out of town looking for a scenic run while on vacation, the scenic national park offers an ideal landscape. Paved trails throughout the park also make it ideal for runners of any skill level.

SUMMIT2SUMMIT

WHAT: Run the half-marathon over two mountains in Hot Springs National Park.

WHERE: Downtown Hot Springs

COST: Fee for registration

PRO TIP: In recent years this race has sold out fast, so be sure to sign up when online registration opens in April at sparunningfest.com.

If you're a runner of any capacity looking to experience Hot Springs up close and at high speeds, one of the most unique ways to do this is through the Spa Running Festival. This annual race offers four different races, including a half-marathon that takes you over not one but two mountains. How fast can you run 13.1 miles over Hot Springs and West Mountains? As of 2024, Michael Picchini from Boston, Massachusetts, holds the record of completing the race in 1 hour, 15 minutes, and 39 seconds in 2022.

This unique race, known as the Summit2Summit, has been run by racers from all over the country since it began in

---

Other races available in the Spa Running Festival include a 10K, 5K, and kids' race.

Photos courtesy of Aaron Brewer

2015. It was added to the annual Spa 10K, which began in 1982. After the addition of Summit2Summit, the race was rebranded as the Spa Running Festival. It's always held two weekends before Thanksgiving, when the fall foliage in the national park is at its peak, providing a gorgeous race for participants.

HIDDEN SPRING

Is there a hidden thermal spring in downtown Hot Springs?

Seeing and feeling the average 143-degree thermal water springs in Hot Springs is the goal of many visitors. The thermal water display spring in Arlington Park is one of the most popular springs that attract people, as it can be seen by passers driving and walking by. People love this spring because it's one of the only places you can access the spring water in a natural setting. Because of this, it tends to be overcrowded, especially during the summer months when many visitors are here on vacation.

There is, however, one display spring that is a little more hidden, therefore unknown to anyone who hasn't done their research. You can come here even on downtown's busiest days and there's a good chance you'll have this spring that's hidden in plain sight to yourself.

To get there, look between the Maurice and Fordyce Bathhouses and you will see the original entrance to Hot Springs National Park. Walk up this paved entryway, and as you approach the stairs that will lead you to the Promenade,

SECRET SPRING

WHAT: Feel the thermal water at this lesser-known and -visited spring.

WHERE: Directly behind the Maurice Bathhouse, located at 369 Central Ave.

COST: Free

PRO TIP: This hideout is a perfect place to bring a picnic or a good book.

you will see the spring tucked away to your left, located directly behind the Maurice Bathhouse. There, you may feel the sacred spring water at your own pace, and in your own peace.

You won't get far in the cave-like hole located above the spring, but it's definitely worth checking out.

DOWNFALL OF THE CANOPY

Do you remember the downtown canopy?

In addition to numerous natural disasters, downtown has had to overcome economic struggles over the years. Just like after each natural disaster, the community banded together once again.

After the illegal gambling era ended in 1967, the local economy began to suffer. Over the next decade, downtown Hot Springs tried to stay afloat. One innovative idea was to put up a canopy with lighting and music above the sidewalk on the west side of Central Avenue. Going up in 1972 and coming down in 1986, the canopy was short-lived but would remain infamous to longtime Hot Springs residents.

"What was wrong with the canopy?" Liz Robbins, executive director of the Garland County Historical Society, muses. "It tried for a modern '70s 'vibe' with large orange globes hanging from rectangular wood blocks. Its design clashed with the architectural styles of the 19th- and early 20th-century downtown buildings. The overwhelming public reaction was negative."

In 1982, the Hot Springs Mall (now called Uptown Hot Springs) opened, and large department stores like Dillard's and JCPenney left the downtown area for the new location, yet another hit to downtown Hot Springs.

Downtown merchant Hannah Mills, who moved to Hot Springs in 1978 to open the Hot Springy Dingy, refused the mall's offer to move her business from the area. She was happy

---

"Mike, do you remember the lovely canopy?" "Sure do. It was ugly, and it leaked."—Clyde Covington and Mike Blythe at the Garland County Historical Society, 2023.

with business before the mall, but after the mall, she knew something had to be done. So Mills started and headed the Downtown Merchants Association of Hot Springs, which remains in existence today. Holding citywide meetings at the Majestic Hotel and (literally) painting the town with her husband, David, and other citizens, she began to see an improvement. Mills credits the Downtown Merchants Association and, of course, the downfall of the canopy for the turnaround.

DOWNTOWN POWERS THROUGH

WHAT: Downtown thrives thanks to merchants.

WHERE: Hot Springy Dingy is located at 409 Park Ave.

COST: Costume rentals and accessories range in price.

PRO TIP: Although Hannah and David retired in 2024, their store remains open under new ownership, sitting alongside numerous other local favorites.

Today, downtown is one of Hot Springs's most beautiful areas, drawing in tourists and locals on a daily basis.

As for Hannah and her business, after yet another tragic landslide in 1995, killing one of her employees and closing her store, she moved up the street to Park Avenue, where she and David continued the Hot Springy Dingy until their official retirement in 2024. The two continue to serve in the Park Avenue Community Association (PACA) in an effort to revitalize the area extending from downtown. Given her track record, I'd say the growing area is lucky to have them.

Photo courtesy of Garland County Historical Society

THE OSTRICHES

What happened to the recreational ostrich farm?

Today Whittington Avenue features residential properties facing a lovely parklike median. At the end of the avenue there was once a popular amusement park. Other attractions along the avenue included Tiny Town, the IQ Zoo, the Alligator Farm, and a well-known baseball field. One of the earliest attractions was the Hot Springs Ostrich Farm, which was established here in 1903, although it originally started in California in 1886.

WHITTINGTON PARK

WHAT: Walk the beautiful, serene park that's left.

WHERE: Whittington Ave.

COST: Free

PRO TIP: It's especially beautiful in the fall.

Thomas A. Cockburn (pronounced Coburn) was a Scotland native who moved to Sri Lanka before settling in California in 1883. That is where he started his first ostrich farm. Five years later, he and his wife would move 300 ostriches to San Antonio to start a new farm. While visiting Hot Springs on vacation, Cockburn and his wife would decide to move the farm once again to Hot Springs.

"The birds were transported to Hot Springs in three railroad cars," Clyde Covington wrote in the 2015 Garland County Historical Society *Record*. "The sight of the ostriches being unloaded at the Rock Island Depot on Benton Street [now Convention Boulevard] must have attracted a large crowd, for no ostrich had been seen in Hot Springs previously, much less such a huge number of the exotic birds."

The farm had ostrich races with "jockeys" riding atop the giant birds and had ostrich-pulled carriage rides. But the birds had a purpose beyond entertainment. The farm's primary purpose was to supply feathers to the fashion industry. Every

Photo courtesy of Garland County Historical Society

nine months the birds had their feathers plucked and cut. This drew crowds, too.

The farm was continued after Cockburn's death in 1930 by his son. In 1936, other animals were added. In 1944, the name was changed to the Hot Springs Ostrich and Wild Animal Farm. In 1953, the farm closed. The animals and six remaining ostriches were sold to the Alabama Zoo.

"No vacation in Hot Springs was complete without a trip to Whittington Avenue to see the marvelous birds."—Clyde Covington, the *Record*, 2015.

DE SOTO

Did de Soto really come here looking for the Fountain of Youth?

There's a popular rumor that Hernando de Soto came to Hot Springs in search of the Fountain of Youth, but this idea is rooted in a mix-up of historical facts. For one, it was actually Juan Ponce de León, not de Soto, who famously searched for the Fountain of Youth.

"[In an 1878 issue of *Harper's Weekly*, writer A.] Van Cleef suggested that it was Arkansas, in fact, that Ponce de León was seeking in 1521 when he settled for Florida, that the hot springs were the 'waters of life,' the reality that became fabled as the Fountain of Youth," Wayne Fields said in a 1991 *American Heritage* piece.

"The possibility that Hernando de Soto saw the springs in 1542 continues to be celebrated in promotional literature, often confusing de Soto with the more commercially attractive Ponce de León and even suggesting that de Soto's death, a few months after his 'visit' to the area, would have been averted had he stayed beside these waters."

And here's the real twist to the de Soto story: according to local historian Mark Blaeuer, he likely never even set foot in Hot Springs.

"One fountain in the Fordyce Bathhouse, for instance, depicts a romanticized meeting between the Caddo and

---

"Scholarly research has found no evidence for the Hernando de Soto expedition being in Hot Springs, Arkansas, although it is still publicized in many quarters that he was here in 1541."—Mark Blaeuer.

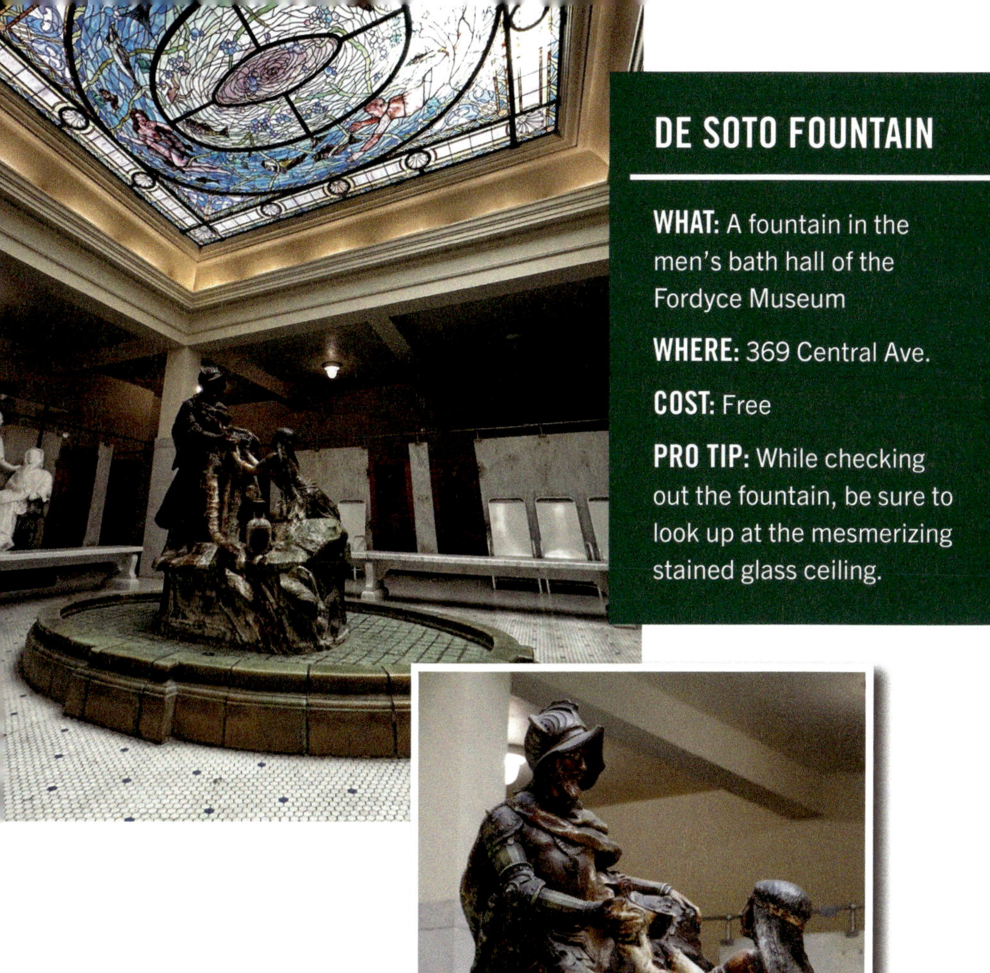

DE SOTO FOUNTAIN

WHAT: A fountain in the men's bath hall of the Fordyce Museum

WHERE: 369 Central Ave.

COST: Free

PRO TIP: While checking out the fountain, be sure to look up at the mesmerizing stained glass ceiling.

Hernando de Soto," Blaeuer writes in his book *Didn't All the Indians Come Here?* "It shows a young woman, possibly the fictional character Ulelah, in a kneeling position, offering him the spring water in a duck effigy bowl. In light of the expedition's unhappy experiences with area tribes . . . the statue says more about relations between sexes and races in 1915–16, when it was installed in the sexually and racially segregated men's bath hall, than about de Soto or American Indians."

KENNY

Who was the local who walked more than 10,000 miles across the country?

Bud Kenny, a multifaceted figure known as an author, adventurer, and downtown businessman, passed away at 71 on October 2, 2019. He founded Wednesday Night Poetry (WNP) in 1989, hosting 1,601 consecutive sessions. Kollective Coffee+Tea is WNP's most recent home, with previous venues including Maxine's, where attendees braved ice storms to maintain the tradition.

Kevin Rogers, former Maxine's owner, praised Kenny's impact in a tribute article in the *Sentinel-Record* on October 4, 2019, likening him to a character from a Bob Dylan song due to his remarkable journeys. These include an 8,000-mile trek on foot from Pennsylvania to Oregon, down the coast to San Francisco, and back across the country to Hot Springs, where his mother was living in 1977 and where he then settled. Another on-foot journey was from Hot Springs to Maine in 2001, chronicled in his book *Footloose in America: Dixie to New England*. He not only traveled on foot during this time but also with a pack donkey.

KENNY'S LEGACY

WHAT: Attend an open mic night at Wednesday Night Poetry.

WHERE: Kollective Coffee+Tea, 110 Central Ave.

COST: Free

PRO TIP: Get there early for a good seat! Gatherings tend to be packed.

In his last years, Kenny was known for his heartfelt connection with his partner, Gin Hartnett, whom he affectionately called his princess, writing countless love poems for her.

Kenny's influence extended beyond poetry, with Kai Coggin, a close friend, describing him as a mentor and father figure. Kenny entrusted Coggin with carrying on WNP's legacy. Despite his passing, Coggin, committed to preserving his poetry community for future generations, says she feels Kenny's

Photos courtesy of Gin Hartnett

presence every Wednesday. Bud Kenny's impact, both through his poetry and personal connections, leaves an indelible mark on all who knew him.

Today, Wednesday Night Poetry continues successfully with having never missed a meeting.

"[Bud was a] disarming tall giant of heart who welcomed everyone young and old to the mic."—Kai Coggin, the *Sentinel-Record*, 2019.

SOUTHERN SAKE

Where can you get locally sourced sake?

Through a relationship with Hanamaki, Japan, in the Hot Springs Sister City Program, Japanese culture has been blending with the Southern society of Hot Springs for nearly three decades. Now, the cultural merge continues as Hot Springs introduces Arkansas's very first sake brewery.

TRY SOUTHERN SAKE

WHAT: Get your hands on some Origami Sake.

WHERE: Visit drinkorigami.com to find it sold in a store near you.

COST: Upward $30

PRO TIP: Visit drinkorigami.com to schedule an in-person tour and tasting at the brewery!

With two years of training in Japan, Arkansas native Ben Bell is the vice president of Origami Sake, alongside President Matt Bell. Together, the two create a Japanese product using Arkansas ingredients—creating a delicious sake of the South.

Origami Sake gets its yamada nishiki rice from Isbell Farms in England, Arkansas—one of two farms in the US that grow this sake rice.

"This is like the cabernet sauvignon of sake rice, except I would say this is more important than cabernet sauvignon is to grapes," Bell told the *Hot Springs Post* in 2022, naming the New York metro area as a large US sake market. However, Bell anticipates that Arkansans will take this on as a local beverage.

As of 2024, you will be hard-pressed not to find a well-stocked bar in Arkansas carrying Origami Sake, many of which have begun making their own signature cocktails with the beverage.

Photos courtesy of Origami Sake

Bell describes sake as both sweet and savory. He said its savoriness is what makes the beverage versatile while pairing with food of even the boldest flavors found in Southern favorites.

BUFFALO DAYS

What happened during the buffalo days?

Hot Springs made national news on April 16, 2015, when six buffalo escaped from the inner-city farm of local resident Tony Bettis, located off of the Hot Springs Creek Greenway Trail. The animals separated and roamed freely through town, creating a spectacle that many residents later described as a quintessential "only in Hot Springs" moment.

"On occasion, we have had some cows escape. I have not heard in my 20 years (in Hot Springs) of buffalo," Hot Springs Police Cpl. Sonia Luzader said in an article published by the *Sentinel-Record* the following day.

The bizarre event inspired the city's tourism office to host the first Buffalo Days festival in April 2016, featuring performances by big names like Bobby Bones, Lauren Alaina, and Uncle Kracker. However, the escape that turned out to have serious consequences for the buffalo had a short-lived celebration, and never returned for a second year.

On the day of the escape, one buffalo was hit by a car, resulting in a fatal hip injury. Within the next 24 hours, three

WHERE THE BUFFALO ROAM

WHAT: Visit the Hot Springs Creek Greenway Trail. Near Shady Grove Road is where you will be in the vicinity of where the buffalo roamed.

WHERE: 780 Adams St.

COST: Free

PRO TIP: The buffalo reportedly started their journey down Shady Grove Road and scattered in different directions. While the farm is private property, it is near the Hot Springs Creek Greenway Trail.

The buffalo days in Hot Springs are absurd and quirky, yet heart-wrenching and tragic.

Photo courtesy of Richard Rasmussen

more were contained. But it would be 18 days until Bettis found one dead, and six more days until the sixth and final buffalo was found in a corral, also deceased. Today, reminders of the buffalo remain in Bettis's home, where taxidermy pieces of the animals are displayed in remembrance of his pets.

What began as an absurd moment of local lore ended as a poignant chapter in Hot Springs history, combining humor, tragedy, and the quirky events that seem to always find a way to unfold in Hot Springs, Arkansas.

MAJESTIC BURNING

What happened to the Majestic Hotel?

The old Army and Navy General Hospital and Medical Arts Building aren't the only abandoned structures still standing with an exquisite history in Hot Springs. But there is one structure that remains only in the memories of locals and serves as a reminder of the importance of restoring historic icons.

Prior to its burning in February 2014, the Majestic Hotel stood abandoned since 2006 at the north end of Central Avenue where it intersects with Whittington and Park Avenues in downtown Hot Springs. Its history, controversy surrounding its use after closing, and what some might consider a suspicious burning are what create great intrigue.

THE BURNING HISTORY OF THE MAJESTIC

WHAT: Convoluted history and fate surrounding the Majestic Hotel

WHERE: 101 Park Ave.

COST: Free

PRO TIP: Watch *Forever Majestic* at forevermajesticfilm.com.

"This sprawling complex had four different buildings," Garland County Historical Society Executive Director Liz Robbins said. "The 1902 yellow-brick one replaced an 1888 Majestic. In 1926 the red-brick Majestic Annex was built. The three-story Lanai Suites were added in 1958, and the 10-story Lanai Towers section was added in 1963."

The Majestic and Arlington hotels were the two big resort hotels that welcomed and pushed for family tourism. They weren't just trying to attract people to come here to take the baths for medicinal purposes. Compared to the Arlington's party scene, the Majestic was very quiet, fancy, and relaxing.

"Financial problems led to the closing of some of the properties in 2004, and the complex was completely closed in 2006," Robbins continues. "Despite subsequent owners, the properties remained abandoned and deteriorating."

Photo courtesy of John Cooksey

The yellow-brick part of the Majestic properties was destroyed by fire on February 27, 2014. It was assumed to have been accidentally started by one of the many homeless people sheltering in the abandoned building, but mentions of teenagers seen trespassing onto the property the night of the fire have also been made.

"The Majestic buildings were at the center of a debate before the fire," Robbins said. "At the time of the Majestic fire, the city wanted to demolish the abandoned structures while a group of activists fought to save them."

After the fire, the rest of the hotel complex was boarded up and condemned until finally demolished by the City of Hot Springs in 2016.

"The burning, although extremely terrible to lose such a piece of architecture in Hot Springs, it was a necessary spark," Michael Schwarz, a leading Majestic activist and filmmaker of the feature documentary *Forever Majestic*, said. "That fire was the spark that really got people to wake up and say, hang on a second, we need to do something about these historic structures we have before they go away."

As of the writing of this book, the lot sits empty, although amphitheaters and hotels have been considered for the space.

The yellow-brick Majestic in 1902 replaced an 1882 Majestic, which had originally been called "The Avenue."

THE ARCH

What's the difference between Fountain Lake and Fountain Lake?

Today, Fountain Lake is only a suburb of Hot Springs, sitting between Hot Springs and Hot Springs National Park. Near the Fountain Lake School District stands a grand white stucco archway established in 1933 that has piqued the curiosity of many who aren't natives to the area for years. Originally developed by Dr. H. D. Ferguson, the property beyond the archway flourished until 1949 as Fountain Lake, an entertainment hub four miles from Hot Springs. Having picnic spots, a sprawling swimming pool, a dance pavilion, cozy lodges, quaint cottages, a whimsical wishing well, a lively pinball arcade, and spectacular July Fourth fireworks, Fountain Lake drew crowds of up to 2,000, as recounted by local historian Bill Lerz.

The Welchman family assumed ownership in 1945, but tragedy struck on a December morning in 1953 when a devastating fire consumed the property, leaving it in ruins. Despite plans from the Arkansas Sheriffs' Association for a

Photo courtesy of Michael Schwarz

potential boys' ranch and subsequent plans in 1962 by Arbordale Springs, Inc. to transform the area into a Lutheran senior citizens' home, these aspirations remained unfulfilled.

Today, the 157-acre Fountain Lake resort, now owned by Affiliated Foods of Little Rock since 1993, has five springs producing over a million gallons of water daily. Passing by, one might witness tanker trucks transporting this spring water to Little Rock, where it's bottled as Mountain Pure Drinking Water.

FOUNTAIN LAKE

WHAT: Learn what's behind the arch.

WHERE: Around 4071 Park Ave.

COST: Free

PRO TIP: While this site is privately owned, you can still visit it virtually. Check out the ruins at abandonedar.com, and for a full-color documentary look up *Hot Springs Arkansas 1939* by @miles8775 on YouTube.

Photo courtesy of Garland County Historical Society

Photo courtesy of Michael Schwarz

The historic remains of Fountain Lake's entertainment hub hold charm, while a nearby town of the same name features Fountain Lake Schools and a shopping center.

THE BIG GUY

Who was Al Capone to Hot Springs?

To the world, Al Capone had a reputation of being "a murderous thug without remorse." But to the people of Hot Springs, Capone was simply "The Big Guy." Today, many historical tributes to this infamous gangster's time spent vacationing here from 1920–1929 can be found.

Capone's first trip to Hot Springs is thought to have been in the fall of 1920 with his boss, the Chicago Southland gang's leader, Johnny Torrio. Checking into the Eastman Hotel under the alias "Al Brown," this would be the first of many times that Capone, then 22, would come to Hot Springs for a "quiet vacation."

After a few stays in the Eastman, Capone began staying in the newly rebuilt Arlington Hotel on his visits. Always in Suite 443, his room at the Arlington had a perfect view of his favorite place to gamble: the Southern Club (now the Josephine Tussaud Wax Museum).

Besides gambling and partying, other activities Capone indulged in while vacationing were visiting the Happy Hollow amusement park, golfing, and soaking in the thermal waters in an attempt to cure his syphilis.

"A visiting gang would send an emissary to the Hot Springs Police Department to notify them that the gang would be in town for a few days," Orval Allbritton writes in his book *Mob at the Spa*. "Most often a 'contribution' was made to the Policemen's Benevolent Fund.

Photo courtesy of the Garland County Historical Society

"Also, after the election of Mayor Leo P. McLaughlin in 1927, a courtesy call was made on him. Capone had sent a contribution to McLaughlin's campaign fund. . . . The mayor supposedly told several of the gang in the Arlington's dining room, *Fellows, enjoy your stay. Spend your money and have a good time. Don't bother the locals. If you get in trouble and get arrested and can't get out of jail, give me a call and I'll come down and get in jail with you.* His statement was greeted with much laughter and backslapping."

VISIT THE SOUTHERN CLUB

WHAT: The old Southern Club is where the Josephine Tussaud Wax Museum is today. Visit the gambling exhibit in the museum.

WHERE: 250 Central Ave.

COST: Fee for admission

PRO TIP: At the end of a tour through the wax museum, you will be taken to an area and told you're looking at a secret tunnel used by Capone. See the "Secret Tunnels" entry in this book for more on that!

"The locals wanted to help Al and his gang to enjoy their stay whenever Capone and the boys visited the Spa City."—Orval Allbritton, *The Mob at the Spa.*

GHOST ADS

Can you spot downtown's ghost ads?

Some art in Hot Springs has been accidental. In the parking lot of Mountain Valley Spring Co., remnants of old advertisements painted onto the wall of 128 Central Avenue can be seen. But what do you see? An ad for 10-cent Tom Moore Cigars? Perhaps the five-cent Coca-Cola ad? Look at the wall in the right light and you may make out the words "SELZ," "Miller," or "$3.50 Royal Blue Shoes."

These ghost ads, which sit protected in the historic district, feature advertisements from approximately 1891 to about 1905. The only reason they have been so well preserved over the years is that a building was erected next to them in the early 1900s, protecting the wall from nature's elements. It wouldn't be until that building was torn down in the late 1980s that the mural would be rediscovered.

Over the past three decades, the mural has changed dramatically due to the sun slowly uncovering all the ads that have been painted on the wall. A few years ago, it was easy

DIVE DEEPER

WHAT: Explore Hot Springs's history deeper next door.

WHERE: Mountain Valley Spring Co., 150 Central Ave.

COST: Free

PRO TIP: Tour the museum and don't forget to grab a few bottles of the iconic green bottled spring water before you leave!

Depending on the year and time of day, every time you look at this mural, you may discover something different. This piece of history is the epitome of leaving art "up to interpretation."

to spot "Tom Moore 10¢ Cigar." But now, that has faded and "Drink Coca-Cola" is more visible. The word "SELZ" can be seen between the windows, with some thinking it reads "SEIZ," a local sign company founded in 1908.

The current building owner placed a sign by the mural describing the different ads at the approximate years they were displayed. This signage states that the neighboring building was erected in 1915. If that is the case, "SELZ" could be "SEIZ." However, according to archived photos found at Garland County Historical Society, the building covering the signage was erected circa 1905, three years before SEIZ was founded.

SISTERS

Who is Hot Springs's sister city?

Origami Sake is just one example of the culture brought to Hot Springs through the Sister City Program. Since January 15, 1993, Hot Springs has held a sister city relationship with Hanamaki, Japan.

A sister city relationship is a long-term partnership between two communities across borders. These entities pursue activities such as municipal, business, trade, education, and cultural exchanges. Relationships develop from diverse sources including preexisting ties, historical connections, demographic links, shared challenges, and personal experiences. In the case of Hot Springs, that's what we have in common with Hanamaki: *hot springs*.

SEE THE CHERRY BLOSSOMS

WHAT: Annual celebration of Japanese culture

WHERE: Hot Springs Convention Center

COST: Free to attend

PRO TIP: Want to try your hand at the festival's haiku competition? Submit an entry!

Both relying heavily on tourism as a primary source of revenue, Hanamaki, like Hot Springs, is also renowned for its bathhouses (*onsen*) fed by local thermal springs, scenic surroundings of rolling hills, and a nearby mountain range. The city's artistic heritage, marked by the presence of acclaimed poet Miyazawa Kenji and numerous other artists, adds to its cultural allure.

While visiting Hanamaki may not be feasible for everyone, Hot Springs offers a taste of its beauty and culture in areas like the Garden of the Pine Wind and the Sunrise Bridge. There is also an exhibit displayed in the Hot Springs Convention Center that showcases contemporary Japanese folk art and a famed

Photos courtesy of Hot Springs Sister City

Deer Dancer costume symbolizing Hanamaki's culture. This costume, a gift from Hanamaki to Hot Springs, was presented during the convention center's grand opening in December 1998.

Hot Springs's Cherry Blossom Festival, a highlight of these festivities, celebrates Japanese culture through music, dance, food, and arts, providing residents of Hot Springs a glimpse into Hanamaki's heritage.

VER HEILL OK SÆLL

Why are those Vikings biking?

Ver heill ok sæll is an Old Norse greeting said to be used by Vikings. It means "to be healthy and happy." Healthy and happy are exactly what these biking Vikings you see in Hot Springs every November exude.

Embracing a playful Viking theme purely for the fun of it rhyming with the activity, this three-day festival is a must for mountain biking enthusiasts. Held annually, the Güdrun – Northwoods MTB Festival transforms the scenic trails of Hot Springs into a vibrant playground for bikers of all skill levels.

The festival kicks off with the Slow Roll Fun Ride, a relaxed ride that welcomes participants to the event and allows them to take in the beautiful surroundings at a leisurely pace. For those seeking more of a challenge, the Full Enduro and Mini Enduro races offer thrilling competition across diverse terrain.

Photo courtesy of Kai Caddy

One of the festival's highlights is the Waffles & Coffee Time Trial, where riders fuel up on delicious waffles and coffee before hitting the trails to race against the clock. This unique combination of food and competition sets a cheerful tone for the day. The excitement continues with the Jump Jam, an event that showcases impressive aerial skills as riders perform jumps and tricks. The Dual Slalom adds another layer of intensity, pitting riders head-to-head in a race down parallel tracks.

In addition to these main events, Güdrun features a variety of other activities and competitions designed to keep both participants and spectators entertained. Whether you're an avid mountain biker or just looking to enjoy the festive atmosphere, there's something for everyone.

Photo courtesy of Visit Hot Springs

SEE YOU AT THE GÜDRUN!

WHAT: Viking-themed mountain biking festival

WHERE: Hot Springs Northwoods

COST: Ranges

PRO TIP: You will most definitely want to dress for the occasion. *Skål*!

The Viking theme adds distinctive fun to Güdrun, making it a standout in Hot Springs. With thrilling races, delicious food, and spirited camaraderie, Güdrun promises an unforgettable experience for all.

GARVAN

Who is the woman behind Garvan Gardens?

Garvan Woodland Gardens is a stunning botanical garden, with pine trees providing cover, waves lapping along 4.5 miles of forested shore, and rocky inclines echoing the nearby Ouachita Mountains. While this is a place adored by visitors and locals alike, few know of the woman behind the garden: Verna Cook Garvan.

VERNA'S LEGACY

WHAT: See Garvan Woodland Gardens.

WHERE: 550 Arkridge Rd.

COST: Fee for admission

PRO TIP: Buy your tickets online to save $5. In the winter, check out the stunning holiday light display.

Verna was an influential figure in Arkansas, known for her clever business sense and philanthropy. She owned the Wisconsin & Arkansas Lumber Company and the Malvern Brick and Tile Company but is best remembered as the founder of Garvan Gardens.

A native of Groveton, Texas, she grew up in Malvern, where her father managed the family businesses. Verna attended Holton-Arms, a girls' school in Washington, DC, with her sister Dorothy. She married Alonzo "Lonnie" B. Alexander in 1934, but after the tragic death of their son Arthur, they divorced in 1956.

Returning to Malvern, Verna took over the family businesses. She married Patrick Garvan Jr. in 1960 and settled in Hot Springs. Despite Patrick's death in 1972, Verna

---

Verna's legacy lives on through the natural beauty and educational opportunities provided by Garvan Woodland Gardens.

continued her agricultural endeavors, which culminated in the creation of Garvan Woodland Gardens on Lake Hamilton.

Verna Garvan's dedication to the gardens led her to establish an endowment agreement with the University of Arkansas, ensuring their maintenance after her passing in 1993. One of her notable contributions to the gardens is the Verna Cook Garvan Pavilion, codesigned by architect E. Fay Jones.

Photos courtesy of Garvan Gardens

NO WAY DANAE

ENJOY THE ART

WHAT: Admire Brissonnet's work.

WHERE: 110 Central Ave.

COST: A cup of award-winning tea costs upwards $4.

PRO TIP: Look closely at the mural. Can you find Graham's dog, Dixie? How about the naked woman handing the man an apple in the thermal waters? Don't forget to stop in at Dee Graham's shopping boutique next door to Kollective before leaving!

Where did the uniquely psychedelic mural neighboring the Catholic church come from?

For anyone entering downtown Hot Springs from Park or Whittington Avenues, an eye-catching colorful mural greets passersby. You would never suspect the controversy behind its inception that resulted in a local art boon.

On the wall of Kollective Coffee+Tea, facing a lawn owned by St. Mary of the Springs Catholic Church, building owner Bobby Graham, with the help of Mary Zunick, commissioned Canadian artist Danae Brissonnet to beautify the side of his building in 2022. The artist's original design included much of the whimsy seen today but also had elements paying homage to historic fires in Hot Springs and the healing thermal waters.

The church expressed dismay about this trippy design, and with the building being in the historic district, some members of the public did as well. Graham, who privately commissioned the piece with help from the Downtown Association, listened to the outcries of the church, and Brissonnet agreed to eliminate the fire element and the flower-headed figure soaking its feet in the water.

In April 2022, Brissonnet came to town, along with other artists, and downtown Hot Springs was painted. In addition to her mural on Kollective, during her time here, Brissonnet worked with local children to create a mural that now stands in David F. Watkins Memorial Park. She was also commissioned by SQZBX Brewery & Pizza to create a mural on the restaurant's back patio. Central Theatre owner Chris Rix commissioned artist Jason Botkin, who came to town with Brissonnet, to create a mural on the front of the historic theater. As Botkin worked, numerous community artists simultaneously created a mural alongside the left wall of the building.

Downtown was splashed with color, artists were empowered, building owners expressed their right to decorate as they please, and any dismayed opinions faded over time.

Photo courtesy of Richard Rasmussen

DOLL TEST

Who was the Hot Springs native who conducted the world-famous "doll test"?

The "doll test" is a famous psychological experiment that took identical dolls, only differing in skin color, and placed them in front of Black children ages 3 to 7 in public schools. Asked to play with them, the children preferred the White dolls, assigning positive characteristics to them and negative characteristics to the Black dolls. Results from the experiment (which showed that segregation resulted in low self-esteem and inferiority complexes among Black children) were an influential part of the testimony considered by the US Supreme Court in its unanimous 1954 decision in the case of Brown v. Board of Education of Topeka. The court's historic decision led to the desegregation of public schools.

WHAT THE CHILDREN TOLD US

WHAT: Tim Spofford's book on Clark

WHERE: Purchase from the Garland County Historical Society.

COST: Fee

PRO TIP: Spofford has another story published in the 2024 Garland County Historical Society *Record* about another highly accomplished member of Clark's family from Hot Springs. Pick up a copy from GCHS.

Although seemingly simple, the experiment was groundbreaking. Its creator was 1934 Langston High School graduate Dr. Mamie Phipps Clark, a native of Hot Springs. In an article by Tim Spofford titled "Dr. Mamie Phipps Clark: Hot Springs Hero Long Overlooked" in the 2023 Garland County Historical Society *Record*, Spofford outlines Clark's Hot Springs roots.

Born October 17, 1917, as Mamie Phipps, her father, Dr. Harold Phipps, was a Caribbean native and her mother, Katie

Photo courtesy of the Garland County Historical Society

Phipps, was a local. Officers of the NAACP, the Phippses raised Mamie and her brother Harold as activists.

At the age of 16, Phipps graduated from Langston, a local Black school, and left for Washington, DC, to attend Howard University. This was the start of her long journey that would be full of accomplishments in the fight for race equality.

Mamie couldn't attend the White school on her street, use the public library, have the spring water at public fountains—and was growing up in Hot Springs when Gilbert Harris was lynched.

HUMAN BONES UNDER CHURCH

Are there really bones under St. John's?

The week of Halloween in 2020, I had the opportunity to team up with local journalist John Archibald and write a collection of hometown ghost stories for the *Sentinel-Record*. The following story was included in the series. It's the one about human bones rumored to be found under St. John the Baptist Catholic Church.

Located at 589 West Grand Avenue is a beautiful Catholic church sitting atop a hill. Its interior matches its exterior beauty with elaborate paintings and sculptures decorating the sanctuary. However, rumor has it the church was built atop a cemetery, and in an effort to honor the dead, remains found during construction were sealed into the altar.

The location may have been Mountain Brook Cemetery in the 1800s, a pauper's cemetery for those who came to Hot Springs in search of healing in the thermal waters and died here as strangers.

On April 28, 2012, Archibald wrote in *Arkansas Catholic*, "All of the graves were removed prior to the construction of St. John Church. However, a local tall tale persists that some of the graves remain under the church. The legend is attributed to a misunderstanding of Catholic teaching. Catholic churches are required to have the relic of a saint placed in the altar. Father West confirmed there aren't any indigent graves under the altar."

A story no one may ever know the truth behind.

GO SEE ST. JOHN'S

WHAT: Check out this marvel atop the hill.

WHERE: 589 W Grand Ave.

COST: Free

PRO TIP: Go during the day so you can see its grand exterior well.

This statement may lead one to believe that it is a mere local tall tale. Except the Garland County Historical Society has one handwritten note in its possession that makes you question everything.

"When ground was broken for St. John's, graves were found, and Wersitzka had a big box built and remains were put in it and cemented, and it is under altar railing at St. John's," Mary J. Roehm Nee Wersitzka, daughter of architect Louis Wersitzka, who built St. John's, wrote in 1911.

MAXINE TEMPLE JONES

Is Hot Springs's most popular bar a former brothel?

Dora Maxine Temple was born in 1917 near Warren, Arkansas, but many just know her as Madam Maxine. There are outrageous stories of this tall, booming woman who dominated the town's prostitution business, and a lot of those stories are told in her book, *Call Me Madam*. The stories are fun, and the bar Maxine's at the corner of Central and Prospect Avenues downtown is also fun, but here's what we know about the woman who was Madam Maxine.

MADAM MAXINE

WHAT: Hot Springs's toughest broad

WHERE: Maxine's is at 700 Central Ave.

COST: *Call Me Madam* can be purchased up the street in the Gangster Museum of America

PRO TIP: Head to Maxine's on one of their burlesque or variety show nights for some good pizza and fun!

"Maxine . . . Jones, an imposing six-foot amazon, was probably the all time 'champion' brawler, and was dubbed the 'Blonde Bomber,'" Orval Allbritton writes in his book *Leo and Verne: The Spa's Heyday*.

The essence of her character is best captured in the story of a night when a male client began complaining and berating one of Maxine's girls.

"When the man became threatening, Maxine knocked him through a door and down some steps," Allbritton writes. "But he wasn't to escape so easily. She followed the man into the yard and picking up a 2 x 4 piece of lumber began to beat the man who tried to get away by crawling under a porch and screaming at the top of his voice, 'Someone please call the police.' Only the intervention of police officers prevented serious injuries from occurring to the 'John.'"

Photo courtesy of Robert Raines

It's not what you do but how you do it!
Maxine, 1954

Allbritton goes on to say that Maxine became too confrontational for Hot Springs authorities, and she was always at odds with the circuit judge, P. E. Dobbs.

"One night at the gate of her 'ranch' she stopped the Garland County Sheriff from entering her premises with a shotgun. She was already in trouble with law enforcement authorities. This did nothing to change their opinion of Maxine. She had lost any support she ever had and her time in Hot Springs ran out. She was sentenced to the State Penitentiary on a drug charge, which she claimed was a 'frame.'"

Maxine operated two brothels in Hot Springs, and a "ranch" outside the city limits. One of her brothels was landlorded by Mayor Leo McLaughlin. She had a reputation for being "rowdy."

HAUNTED ARLINGTON

What happens in the Capone Suite?

Of all the stories told about the Arlington and its rich history throughout this book, it won't come as any big surprise that it's rumored to be totally haunted. In a 2020 interview with the *Sentinel-Record*, Arlington Director of Operations Carmen Jones tells all, starting with the fact that prior to around 2015, hotel employees were discouraged from sharing their haunting experiences with others. The thought was it would scare off guests. Little did they know it would make the hotel a highly desired haunted destination for visitors.

Working at the Arlington since 1997, Jones has stories of her own and countless tales from guests to back up the claims of this being a haunted hotel. Many of these stories come from suite 443, which is the suite infamous gangster Al Capone stayed in while visiting Hot Springs.

Guests frequently report eerie incidents in the Capone Suite, including the smell of a cigar burning in this now nonsmoking hotel and moving doorknobs. This isn't the only area of the hotel where potentially haunted incidents have occurred, but it is the area that has had the most witnesses to said incidents.

One of the more minor offenses is the unexpected flickering and dimming lights in the Magnolia and Venetian dining rooms. In room 824, guests have experienced lights flickering around 3 to 4 a.m.

"This particular bathroom, the sink will turn on periodically and the bathroom will get all steamy while they're asleep, and

---

Another haunting can be found in the hotel's men's bath hall where a man resembling a soldier taking a bath has been seen for decades.

they wake up and they walk in there and their items fall off the shelves," Jones said.

On the seventh floor, there has been photographic evidence of the haunting experience.

"I've heard several stories . . . of where you see an image of a lady in a white gown walking, and there's a photograph I have, and there's no way there's any type of light, but it looks like there's two footprints on the carpet," Jones said. "It's pretty creepy."

These footprints were in front of room 723.

STAY WITH CAPONE

WHAT: Will you encounter Capone in his favorite suite?

WHERE: The Arlington Resort Hotel & Spa, 239 Central Ave.

COST: The Capone Suite costs upwards $400.

PRO TIP: The Capone Suite is the most popular suite at the Arlington, so be sure to book well in advance.

SPY CATS

Were spy cats trained on Bathhouse Row?

When I came to Hot Springs as a 22-year-old journalist, this story is what made me fall in love with writing about Hot Springs. It encapsulates the quirkiness and connectedness this small town has to the rest of the world. It follows the unique life of Bob Bailey, assistant technical director of Hot Springs's famed IQ Zoo that showcased trained animals doing human tasks. But the IQ Zoo was just one of many animal training ventures Bailey had.

From being the director of the first US Navy Marine Mammal Program to training spy cats for the CIA on Hot Springs's Bathhouse Row, the old pro has a few unbelievable stories to tell. The story that garnered the most attention from my burning little ears was the one where the CIA contacted Bailey to help train train a group of cats intended to spy on the Soviets in the Cold War.

These felines with microphones embedded in their ears were given to the minds behind the IQ Zoo to be trained. And what better place to train them than on Bathhouse Row?

"The CIA hoped that the cats would someday walk near suspected Russian targets and the microphones in cats' ears would broadcast the suspects' conversations to out-of-sight CIA agents," Garland County Historical Society Executive Director Liz Robbins explains.

The team with the zoo leased the top floors of buildings along the west side of Central Avenue and from them used an

ANIMALS IN HOT SPRINGS TODAY

WHAT: The IQ Zoo is long gone, but there is another type of zoo in Hot Springs.

WHERE: The Arkansas Alligator Farm & Petting Zoo is located at 847 Whittington Ave.

COST: Fee for admission

PRO TIP: The IQ Zoo may be gone, but videos of the trained animals can be found on YouTube.

Photos courtesy of the Garland County Historical Society

ultrasonic signal to control the felines on the sidewalk across the street. This went on for years and no one ever knew it.

In 2013, *Smithsonian* magazine featured Bailey's work with these spy cats. Soon after, Smithsonian Network contacted him to create a TV series blending James Bond with cats.

"I wouldn't have anything to do with it; I wouldn't touch it with a 10-foot pole," Bailey told me in 2019 as I wrote his story for the *Sentinel-Record*. "They wanted to be too sensational, and I don't like to sensationalize. It's interesting enough by itself."

Throughout his career, Bailey has trained thousands of different animals, from cockroaches to killer whales.

SWEET CHEWAUKLA

What is Guy Lombardo's tribute to Hot Springs?

The ruins of the Chewaukla Bottling Factory still stand on Sleepy Valley Road today as a thing of beauty. But what about the lore behind this crumbling structure? I'll tell you, it's a good story involving an Native American princess and Guy Lombardo.

The story begins when a chieftain came to Hot Springs looking for healing in the thermal waters. Unfortunately, the hot waters did not help him.

"After bathing in the pools, immersing himself in hot mud, and enduring the sweat tepee, his condition did not improve," Sandra Long said in a February 9, 1992,

SEE THE RUINS

WHAT: See the ruins of the Chewaukla Bottling Factory.

WHERE: Near 515 Sleepy Valley Rd.

COST: Free

PRO TIP: The Chewaukla Bottling Factory is private property that shouldn't be explored up close. However, you can see the ruins from the road particularly well when the greenery has died off in the fall and winter.

Photo courtesy of Michael Schwarz

Photo courtesy of the Garland County Historical Society

Photo courtesy of Michael Schwarz

Sentinel-Record article. "His illness worsened and his pain grew so severe that he could not sleep." As Long recounts the tale in the local newspaper, she says the chieftain's daughter wept for his pain as he became delirious. She came to her father's teepee, and led him to where she hoped would be the rumored magical cool waters outside of the valley that could cure him. "After passing through a deep gorge in the mountain, they followed a small stream until they reached a place where five cool, living springs burst forth from the rocky earth," Long writes. "Here, the princess made her father drink. When he awoke, his pain was gone and he was cured of his affliction. Out of gratitude to his lovely daughter, the chief gave her name to the springs and they were known thereafter as Chewaukla Springs, which meant 'Sleepy Water.'"

The sleepy water soon became famous for the relaxing effect it had on all who drank there, and in the 1930s the Chewaukla Bottling Factory you see remnants of today was built. And so began the nationwide promotion of the water that "retains and regains health" with its slightly alkaline nature.

One of the bottling company's most impressive advertising gimmicks was a song by Guy Lombardo recorded in New York, March 20, 1929, "Sweet Chewaukla–Land of Sleepy Water."

PEST-95

What came before COVID-19?

In 1895, Hot Springs saw a smallpox epidemic that shows a staggering resemblance to how society handled the more recent COVID-19 pandemic.

The Pest
IS GONE—
Spring Is Here!
So Is Our—
..NEW GOODS..
Like Spring Flowers We Have Them In Profusion.
A Beautiful Assortment.
A Complete Assortment!

Photo courtesy of the Garland County Historical Society

During the 1895 smallpox epidemic, public health officials faced significant challenges in addressing the outbreak. Despite efforts to suppress the disease, societal tensions and economic hardships complicated their response. Vaccination efforts were opposed, and quarantine measures appeared to favor the wealthy and middle class, allowing them to leave town at the onset of the epidemic while other cities had already quarantined against Hot Springs. Political tensions, exacerbated by an election during the epidemic, further complicated the situation.

Local news accounts and private correspondence from the period indicate the establishment of an isolation hospital, referred to as a "pest house" near the city. Houses infested with smallpox were marked, and some individuals were sent to the isolation hospital. However, not all infected people made it to the hospital, suggesting challenges in containment efforts.

It's true what they say: history repeats itself. Unfortunately, lessons tend to not stand the test of time.

Evidence suggests that indigents and marginalized populations were disproportionately affected, with some buried in pauper grave sites in the "pest cemetery."

Despite these challenges, physicians and officials worked to suppress the epidemic, enlisting the help of various medical professionals and acquiring vaccination supplies. Eventually, control measures were implemented, including quarantine, inoculation, inspection, and containment efforts. The epidemic, which lasted for several months, greatly harmed the local tourist economy.

The Pest House (aka City Hospital for Contagious Diseases) eventually burned, but its adjoining cemetery (called City Cemetery) was used as a paupers' graveyard until 1983. The cemetery was placed on the National Register of Historic Places in 1921.

PEST HOUSE CEMETERY

WHAT: Can you find this abandoned cemetery?

WHERE: Adams St.

COST: Free

PRO TIP: Go to findagrave.com to find coordinates. Can you find the few markers left at the Pest Cemetery?

TINIEST TOWN

Which business has taken 11 hits via car?

Tiny Town, a family-owned local mainstay, combines charm, tradition, and perhaps a little bad juju. Being hit 11 times by vehicles flying down Whittington Avenue, the Moshinskies' niche business has shown nothing less than astounding perseverance. In fact, it was disaster that brought the attraction to Hot Springs in 1962.

As a teenager in the 1930s, Frank Moshinskie, father to current owner Charles Moshinskie, took great pleasure in tinkering and building miniature cities to surround the train track that decorated the bottom of his Christmas tree. One year, he decided to leave the display up after the holidays and continued to build onto the city. The growing tiny town eventually began to garner attention from the neighborhood, creating a popular hangout spot in Moshinskie's Louisiana home. Unfortunately, in 1962 disaster struck. It was a tornado that would rip the roof off of the building housing Moshinskie's tiny town. However, it was the insurance money resulting from that disaster that would allow him to move the attraction to the tourism community of Hot Springs.

Tiny Town visitors will travel through a 1960s foreward America, without leaving the single room Tiny Town sits in. Walked around the perimeter of the custom built platform by Moshinskie or his wife, you will see icons from Dolly Parton to Michael Jackson, and landmarks like Mount Rushmoore. And you may not believe all of the art before you has been created from what most would consider "garbage." Interactive

TINY TOWN

WHAT: Visit Tiny Town.

WHERE: 374 Whittington Ave.

COST: Fee for admission

PRO TIP: Can you find the tiny Willie Nelson?

with moving belts, rotating platforms, running water features, flickering lights, and even a plane soaring above the town, Tiny Town is undoubtedly unlike anything you've ever seen.

After the 11th collision, the city installed boulders between the Tiny Town building and Whittington Avenue. There has not been another crash since July 2016.

FUNERAL TO GO

Was there really a drive-through funeral home with a brothel upstairs?

One peculiar happening surrounding the dead in Hot Springs is the story of the drive-through funeral home that was located at 217 Central Avenue. And on the second floor? A brothel.

Hot Springs was supposedly ahead of its time with the Ledwidge Undertaking Parlor in the early 1900s, as this was not something America really saw until the 1980s. And even then, I can't imagine any of those had a brothel attached.

Ledwidge Undertaking was "modern in every way," Jim Moshinskie writes to flickr.com. "It even included a drive-thru feature in which the hearses and carriages could use a driveway through the middle of the building to reach stables in the rear of the building. Ledwidge [also] operated the first motorized hearse in Hot Springs."

There is not much more to be found on this peculiar multi-business oddity today. There is a plaque outside of the building, marking it as the Ledwidge Funeral Home, and it is talked about on the downtown Haunted Ghost Tour. However, whether it was a drive-through funeral home for carriages to come through and view bodies (as widely rumored), or simply a drive-through entrance as Moshinskie describes, no one now knows.

"Chris J. Ledwidge started his business in 1908 after he purchased the Bentz & Buchanan Undertakers which had operated [on] the first floor of the Hot Springs Opera House since 1883," Moshinskie writes. "He moved the business into this handsome two-story brick building. Paul J. Caruth remained with Mr. Ledwidge as the funeral director/embalmer. Caruth stayed with the Ledwidge firm until 1919 when he left to open his own funeral home at 655 Park Ave."

Caruth Funeral Home remains in operation today.

TAKE A HAUNTED TOUR

WHAT: Haunted downtown tours give you a fun and exaggerated retelling of spooky history.

WHERE: 430 Central Ave.

COST: Fee for tour

PRO TIP: Wear your walking shoes, and call 501-339-3751 for more information.

Ledwidge died on Halloween 1933. His funeral home closed two years later.

PLAY BALL

Is Hot Springs the birthplace of spring training?

The history of America's favorite pastime in Hot Springs started in 1886, and today many people consider it the birthplace of spring training. As Major League Baseball teams faced the challenges of cold northern winters hindering spring training, Albert Goodwill Spalding, president of the Chicago White Stockings, thought to come to Hot Springs for a warmer training.

HIT THE TRAIL

WHAT: Historic Baseball Walking Trail through downtown

WHERE: Start at Whittington Park.

COST: Free

PRO TIP: Make sure your phone is plenty charged so you can use it on this lengthy walking tour. You can take the tour by scanning a QR code or calling in! The information is at hotspringsbaseballtrail.com.

The *Sporting News*, in its premiere issue on March 17, 1886, announced the Chicago White Stockings' bold decision to train in Hot Springs because Spalding and his player-manager Adrian "Cap" Anson sought to send a physically fit team onto the field when the National League season opened in April. The primary motivation behind this trip to Hot Springs was for players to indulge in the thermal waters, believed to cleanse bodies of alcohol, help them shed weight, and enhance their physical conditions. Spalding also believed that in the milder Southern weather, players could get in shape by climbing local mountains.

The floodgates opened after Spalding's decision, drawing major and minor league teams, as well as individual players, to Hot Springs from 1886 to the 1940s. Teams like the Pittsburgh Pirates, Boston Red Sox, Cincinnati Reds, and Brooklyn Dodgers, among others, embraced the Arkansas resort for spring training. Eventually, African American teams followed, including the legendary Kansas City Monarchs and Pittsburgh

Photo courtesy of the Garland County Historical Society

Crawfords. Stars like Satchel Paige and Josh Gibson trained here, marking a pivotal era in the history of Negro League baseball.

The daily life of these baseball stars intertwined with local activities, creating memorable moments like John McGraw's arrest for gambling in 1904 or Honus Wagner officiating a high school basketball game in 1912.

As the decades passed, major league teams gradually shifted their spring training bases to other states, leaving behind a legacy that echoes through the Hot Springs Historic Baseball Trail.

ARKANSAS

Where can you see Hot Springs on the big screen?

There's an episode of the Nickelodeon cartoon *SpongeBob SquarePants* in which his employer, the Krusty Krab, makes a commercial. When the commercial airs, SpongeBob is shown almost completely cut out of the two frames he was in. "That was the best 60 seconds of my life," SquarePants says after the commercial concludes.

This was Hot Springs when it had five minutes of screen time in the movie *Arkansas*, featuring Liam Hemsworth, Vince Vaughn, and Arkansas native Clark Duke.

In the movie, there's a quick glimpse and mention of Centerfold, a local adult entertainment club; a shot of the local bar Maxine's in a montage; a pan over downtown Hot Springs where you see a "Tom Daniel Chili Cook Off" banner; and a longer scene in the Fordyce Bathhouse.

In the Fordyce scene, you can see its iconic stained glass ceiling, the statue of Hernando de Soto, and Liam Hemsworth

HOT SPRINGS GOES HOLLYWOOD

WHAT: The *Arkansas* movie features a glimpse of Hot Springs.

WHERE: Downtown Hot Springs

COST: A tour through the Fordyce Bathhouse museum where the scene was shot is free.

PRO TIP: Stream the movie on Hulu, then go visit the actual sites featured.

Hot Springs had its five minutes of fame in this fictional narrative involving drug lords, but there are a slew of illegal things that *actually* happened in its colorful history of gangsters and gambling.

Photos courtesy of Anthony Valinoti

inside one of the tubs. The scene lasts about five minutes. The rest of the movie was shot mostly in Alabama.

The famed actors came to Hot Springs the week of November 19, 2018, to shoot their scenes. The locals buzzed at the thought—and for a lucky few, the sight—of Hemsworth at iconic Hot Springs locations like Bathhouse Row. It was an exciting day, and as someone who lives in and loves Hot Springs, it was an exciting thing to see it featured in such a prominent movie, even if it was for just a few moments.

The movie follows the life of Kyle (Hemsworth) and Swin (Duke), who are low-level criminals working for an Arkansas drug lord named Frog (Vaughn). This fictional story of crime and mishap is fitting for a place like Hot Springs.

DELICIOUS THERMAL WATER

How can you consume the thermal waters?

Get it while it's hot! Drinking the thermal water is something locals do regularly and visitors have on the top of their to-do lists. There are three different fountains anyone can freely come to and fill up jugs or bottles: in front of the Libbey Memorial Physical Medicine Center on Reserve Street, in front of the National Park Service Administration Building on Reserve Street, and outside the park boundaries at the Hill Wheatley Plaza on Central Avenue.

Some people bring one jug, but most pull their cars up and fill dozens of jugs to take home. From mason jars to recycled milk jugs, I've seen it all.

Many drink and bathe in the water because they believe it has healing properties. The minerals found in the water include calcium, silica, magnesium, sodium, potassium, bicarbonate, sulfate, chloride, fluoride, oxygen, iron, and radon gas.

In a January 12, 2021, article by Robert Pellegrino for *Hot Springs Natural*, he says research shows that minerals like silica in the water help remove aluminum from the body, while also promoting softer skin, shinier hair, stronger nails, and supple joints.

The combination of minerals helps protect against high stomach acid and constipation. Natural oxygen in the water is said to aid exercise recovery, flush toxins out of the body, and improve alcohol metabolism.

TRY IT IN BEER

WHAT: Beer brewed using the thermal water

WHERE: Superior Bathhouse Brewery

COST: The Beer Bath is upwards $40.

PRO TIP: Superior has 18 taps cycling at all times. Try all 18 in a "Beer Bath" flight. (Psst . . . they also have root beer!)

Photo courtesy of Rob Cox

Photo courtesy of the Superior Bathhouse Brewery

You may come across a few cold spring fountains downtown, too. Unlike the thermal waters coming from Hot Springs Mountain, these cold springs are sourced from West and North Mountains. These springs are treated using ozone filtration systems.

"Congress first protected the hot springs in 1832, and it intended for the water to be used."—Hot Springs National Park.

RUSSIAN GINGERBREAD HOUSE

THE VILLA

WHAT: The closest you can get to this private residence

WHERE: 634 Prospect Ave.

COST: Postcards of the residence can be purchased on eBay.

PRO TIP: This is a private residential villa. If you'd like to see it up close, visit the Lawsons on October 31 in your best costume.

Is there a life-size gingerbread house from Russia on Prospect Avenue?

Strolling down Prospect Avenue, one can appreciate many beautiful, historic, and simply unique homes. One that's hard to miss is the Russian Villa. There are many rumors behind this home that looks like a life-size gingerbread house. The most widely believed one is that the home came from Russia.

The story goes like this: in the early 1900s, a deconstructed Russian home was sent to Hot Springs to be rebuilt. Each piece of timber was numbered so it could be reconstructed exactly. The man behind this supposed intense and precise project was Russian immigrant Eugene Wagner.

Bill Lawson, the home's current owner, and his wife, Janis, were unsure of a lot of the details about the home's creation, but they were certain it did not come to Hot Springs in pieces from Russia.

"The wood came from the Ouachita Mountains," Bill states plainly as he recalls inspecting and renovating many areas of the house many times since he purchased it.

Left: *Painting courtesy of artist Alison Parsons*

One piece of the story that does ring true is that it was built by Russian immigrant Eugene Wagner. Unsure of the exact year the home was completed, official documents confirm at the very least that the land was purchased in 1939.

According to *Then and Now: Hot Springs, Arkansas* by Mike Blythe, Wagner, once a colonel in the army of Czar Nicholas II, retired to Hot Springs from Chicago after many years in business there. The Russian Villa was patterned after his childhood home. The home has had many owners since Wagner's death in 1968.

Of those owners, it seems like the integrity of the structure has been best kept by Lawson. When Lawson saw that the house that he had long desired was for sale in 2011, he purchased it for $125,000 and got to work on deconstructing renovations made to it by past owners. One hundred fifty thousand dollars in renovations later, the Russian Villa stands the way Wagner intended it to.

Over the years, different owners renovated the home yet remarkably managed to preserve a piece of history—a mural of Nicholas II, the last emperor of Russia, on a hallway wall.

COLD THERMAL WATER

Will the springs stay hot forever?

In a constant, unprecedented time of climate change, some may wonder: will the hot springs ever go cold? Currently flowing at about 143 degrees, the thermal waters are hot enough to kill harmful bacteria, making it safe to consume. If the temperatures decreased significantly, it would render the springs useless outside of their beauty and be a multilevel devastation to the community.

But these waters have run hot for over 4,000 years. Is it reasonable to think one day they won't? In an August 25, 2021, interview, Hot Springs National Park Natural Resource Program Manager Nathan Charlton said that he thinks it is possible. One reason is extreme weather events causing heavy rainfall.

When precipitation increases, so does flow, and temperatures decrease.

"We have two different types of water that's coming into our springs," Charlton said. "We have the ancient hot water, thermal water that's 4,000 years old that falls as rain in the recharge zone and . . . up to 30 percent can be just regular shallow cold groundwater that mixes with it right before it emerges."

Large rain events increase the amount and speed of groundwater flowing into the springs, causing the temperatures to drop. The decrease in temperatures is monitored regularly;

> Charlton said climate change's current effects are going to eventually impact the health, quality, and quantity of the thermal hot water in Hot Springs, and he feels like this is already evident.

they have only decreased about six degrees before returning to their normal temperature in drier weather.

But if the weather gets too dry, the environment is at risk of drought. Drought leads to an unhealthy forest susceptible to pests, tree death, and wildfire. Fewer trees leads to more runoff, therefore less infiltration, which will reduce the recharge and the flow of the springs.

FEEL THE WATER

WHAT: Test a hot spring for yourself.

WHERE: Arlington Park

COST: Free

PRO TIP: Head up the stairs to the right of the spring for a different view. Go to the top and you'll be at the Promenade!

FORGOTTEN OFFICER

Who was Jack Donahue?

There is one story found in Orval Allbritton's *Hot Springs Gunsmoke* of a man forgotten.

Jack Donahue came to Hot Springs close to the end of the year 1900 at 34 years old. The first week of 1901, he began a job at the Hot Springs Police Department.

"From a review of the existing records it was apparent Jack Donahue was a very active enforcement officer, his name appearing as the arresting officer on almost every page of the police docket for the next several months," Allbritton writes.

Donahue was quickly promoted to chief of detectives. The new Hot Springs local would thrive in this position until December 25, 1902.

Around 4 p.m. on Christmas Day, Donahue was called to arrest a man who was firing a pistol and racing his horse through the city. The perpetrator was eventually revealed to be James Dougherty, a former Kansas policeman gone outlaw. As Donahue approached him, Dougherty shot him point-blank, killing the detective. Dougherty was arrested, and in July 1903, he killed an inmate and committed suicide in jail as he awaited his execution after being convicted of Donahue's murder.

"There was much outrage over Donahue's murder in 1902," Liz Robbins says. "The city paid for Donahue's burial and his family put up (perhaps with donations from grateful citizens) a nine-foot-tall marble obelisk in his honor in Hollywood Cemetery. However, over time he was forgotten—

Donahue has since been placed on the National Law Enforcement Officers Memorial memorial in Washington, DC, and on the list of fallen heroes on the HSPD website.

even by the Hot Springs Police Department.

"In 2006 the Hot Springs Police Department received an inquiry about him, but the city's old payroll records had been destroyed. The department asked the Garland County Historical Society for help. The society's research revealed Donahue's story."

DONAHUE'S GRAVE

WHAT: Can you find the grave?

WHERE: Hollywood Cemetery

COST: Free

PRO TIP: Pay your respects. Leave Donahue some flowers.

VIOLET BOLES

Is the Bathhouse Soapery haunted?

The story of Violet Boles has been haunting Hot Springs over the years in more ways than one.

The story starts with an 18-year-old woman named Violet Boles who worked at the Japanese Tea Room at 366 Central Avenue (now the Bathhouse Soapery) and encountered a man she befriended in school named Elmer Jones. Jones, who was 22 at the time of the incident, wanted to be more than friends, but Boles didn't. Boles was kind to Jones for years, but he grew to be obsessed. The obsession worsened when he came back from World War I injured.

"He was never the same after returning from the war," Jones's father said in a December 3, 1922, statement to the *Sentinel-Record*. "The boy would pace the floor at home in a nervous condition, and was entirely changed in character from what he was before he went to war."

In addition to calling Boles at home constantly, Jones would harass her at her job. This went on until one day Jones fatally shot Boles before turning the gun on himself, inside the Japanese Tea Room on December 2, 1922.

For some, this is just a haunting ghost story. Popularly told on haunted tours and around Halloween, it's become local lore that you can "sense" the ghost of Elmer Jones in the back corner of the Bathhouse Soapery.

In 2016, journalist Max Bryan spoke with Boles's great-niece Kmarie Boles Hearn to give perspective of how the ghost

---

"JEALOUSY CAUSE OF TRAGEDY WHEN YOUTH USES GUN / ELMER JONES KILLS MISS VIOLET BOLES AND HIMSELF / WERE NOT SWEETHEARTS."—The *Sentinel-Record* front-page headline, 1922.

HOT SPRINGS NATIONAL PARK, ARKANSAS

JEALOUSY CAUSE OF TRAGEDY WHEN YOUTH USES GUN

ELMER JONES, KILLS MISS VIOLET BOLES AND HIMSELF.

WERE NOT SWEETHEARTS

Jones Had Called Girl up and Tried to Make Engagements, and When These Were Refused He Shot Her Down as She Was at Her Work.

Another double tragedy was enacted in Hot Springs yesterday afternoon about 4 o'clock in the Japanese Tea Room at 366 Central avenue when Elmer Jones, 22 years of age, walked into the kitchen in the rear of the place and shot and killed Miss Violet Boles, of 516 School street, waitress in the tea room.

Photo courtesy of the Garland County Historical Society

BATHHOUSE SOAPERY

WHAT: Visit the site of the crime.

WHERE: 366 Central Ave.

COST: Grab a bar of homemade soap for upwards $9.

PRO TIP: Can you find the grave sites of Violet and Elmer? Here's a hint: They are in the same vicinity of one another in the Greenwood Cemetery. Look for "Jones" on Elmer's tombstone, because his first name has been scratched almost completely out.

lore repeated in the community has affected her family in a very real way. "This is not a ghost story," Hearn told Bryan in an article published with the *Sentinel-Record* on September 22, 2016. "It is a true story of my family."

Hearn said Boles's death devastated her immediate family. She said her mother didn't even attend the funeral. "It affected her mother for the rest of her life," Hearn said. "The grief never left her. It physically affected her, with her health and her mental state." Hearn said she feels it is important that the story be told, so long as it is told factually.

ADAIR PARK'S HONOR

Who does downtown's Adair Park honor?

A popular rest stop for downtown shoppers with a view and some pretty good busking most days, Adair Park is a beautiful part of the downtown area wedged between two shops. In a book titled *The Challengers: Untold Stories of African Americans Who Changed the System in One Small Southern Municipality*, local author Elmer Beard opens with the story of City Alderman Kenneth Adair, whom this park was named after. In light of the fact that Adair Park is so popular among tourists, it's unsurprising Adair's story is often overlooked by people simply passing through. However, this is a man who was able to leave a prominent footprint in local government, helping to create a more equal environment in the city.

"Before he became an elected official, Adair owned and published a local Black newspaper, *The Arkansas Citizen*," Beard writes. "Adair had used the newspaper, since its inception in 1958, as a platform to advance the less fortunate."

Adair ran for alderman six times before he was first elected. The reason his sixth attempt was a success is because the rule changed from citywide votes for ward aldermen being taken to only citizens within a particular ward being allowed to vote. Adair ran in Ward 3 (known as District 2 today), which is predominantly Black.

In 1985, Adair was serving his seventh two-year term on the Hot Springs City Council.

ADAIR PARK

WHAT: Quaint park in the middle of bustling downtown

WHERE: 354 Central Ave.

COST: Free

PRO TIP: You'll want to plan to stop by Adair Park when shopping downtown, as it's just a "stop by" destination rather than a fully developed park. It's a nice little break and oftentimes has free entertainment on its stage.

During his time as an elected official, Adair suggested the city hire its first jail matron to supervise and attend to female prisoners. He also established a free blood pressure service for citizens. And at his first city council meeting, Adair and Beard (who also served as an alderman) cast the only two dissenting votes on a resolution that the state reinstate the death penalty.

Since Adair, District 2, which contains the Pleasant Street District (a district containing the historic African American community), has remained overseen by Black politicians. Beard went on to become the director of the district for the years to come. Today, Beard's daughter, Phyllis Beard, is the city director overseeing the district.

Left: *Photo courtesy of the Garland County Historical Society*

"He became one of the most outspoken officials the city has ever known."—Elmer Beard, *The Challengers*.

MAGIC OR MAYHEM

What's going on at the Malco?

Another local haunt is the historic Malco Theatre, which houses Maxwell Blade's magic show.

"What old town have we not been to where an old theatre has stories of ghosts, etc.? And we are not immune to that," Blade, also the theater owner, told the *Sentinel-Record* in 2020. "After being here in this building for so many years, we have experienced odd things. Have I seen a ghost? Maybe not, but I think I've heard a ghost a couple of times."

EXPERIENCE THE MALCO

WHAT: Watch Blade's magic show.

WHERE: 817 Central Ave.

COST: Ticket prices vary.

PRO TIP: Head over to the Lounge connected to the theater lobby and ask the bartender about hauntings in the building.

Although never confirmed, there have been four people who have died in the building, one a young boy in an upstairs bathroom. Blade says when his daughter was 3 years old, she stood at the base of the theater's winding staircase, pointed to the empty top, and asked, "Daddy, who's that little boy up there?"

Blade himself has also seen his fair share of "shadow figures" crossing doorways and felt coattail pulls backstage. Guests, too, have experienced hauntings that have led them to "wet themselves," Blade says in the 2020 article.

"In 1999, I left this door open on the top balcony. I was called by the police, I came here," Blade says. "There were six police officers here going through, because it's quite large, to see if someone was in the building.

"They were not, but there were two police officers out back that said to me 'I will never go back in that building as long as I live—ever.' And I said 'Why?' And they just shook their heads and walked away."

Blade has been with the historic building for 27 years, and he's convinced it's haunted.

"Why do I think it's haunted? Why wouldn't it be? It's the perfect spot. . . . It's a fun place. Matter of fact, when I go, this is where I want to hang out."—Maxwell Blade, the *Sentinel-Record*, 2020.

Left and right: *Photos courtesy of Gabby Blade*

MIKE DUGAN

Who was the Majestic Park driver?

Today, Hot Springs has a beautiful five-field baseball complex in place of what used to be a major league spring training venue for greats like Babe Ruth, then a home to Hot Springs's minor league team, and then playing fields for the Boys & Girls Club. Majestic Park attracts Little League, softball, and baseball leagues from across the region and provides a place for local teams to play.

It is a dream come true for any baseball enthusiast. But few know the story of the man behind the curtain. Mike Dugan was a proud Hot Springs native, historian, and lover of all things baseball. He wanted to bring back a local youth baseball league that dissolved with the Boys & Girls Club, and his solution was the creation of Majestic Park.

LET'S PLAY BALL

WHAT: Enjoy an afternoon at the ballpark.

WHERE: 105 W Belding

COST: Ranges

PRO TIP: Stop in for a visit to the park while strolling the scenic Hot Springs Creek Greenway Trail.

Photos courtesy of Susan Dugan

Motivated by pure passion, Dugan campaigned tirelessly to pass a bond issue that would secure $8.5 million for the project and worked with developers to ensure history would be woven throughout the park's design.

Dugan was a husband, father, and friend. Prior to the park's completion in the spring of 2021, Dugan died on February 4, 2021, shortly after being diagnosed with brain cancer. He never got to see his dream come to fruition, but today his legacy lives on in the park he helped create. His widow, Susan, feels his presence there today as she reflects fondly on her husband's desire to see the park come to life.

"He said many times to me, boy, as a young boy to play on the same field that Babe Ruth did . . . it would have been exciting," she said to the *Hot Springs Post*.

Dugan saw the creation of Majestic Park as a three-way benefactor: it preserved the site's history, it gave baseball back to local children, and it helped the economy.

"He was a Hot Springs guy through and through . . . and by God he was going to have the best for his community, and I think when people see the field[s] they'll see that he delivered."—Steve Arrison, Visit Hot Springs CEO.

SMITHSONIAN-WORTHY

What piece of Hot Springs is found in the Smithsonian?

Ron Coleman Mining is more than just a fun activity for visitors and locals alike. Among numerous mines in the state, Ron Coleman Mining stands out for its exceptional specimens, making it a favored destination for quartz enthusiasts.

The Berns Quartz, a remarkable discovery from the mine, has become a centerpiece at the Smithsonian's National Museum of Natural History. Unearthed in 2016 and placed in the museum in 2021, this colossal cluster of quartz crystals, weighing over 8,000 pounds and standing seven feet tall, captivates visitors with its sheer size and beauty.

There are three places to dig for quartz in the country: Little Falls and Ellenville, New York, and Hot Springs, Arkansas.

Named after Michael and Tricia Berns, whose support facilitated its acquisition by the museum, the Berns Quartz holds a place of honor alongside iconic treasures like the Hope Diamond. Its significance extends beyond its visual appeal because it serves as a valuable resource for scientific research and education.

DIG FOR QUARTZ

WHAT: Find impressive specimens for yourself.

WHERE: 211 Crystal Ridge Ln.

COST: Fee for admission

PRO TIP: Bring a plastic rake, bucket, water (for drinking and crystal cleaning), and sunblock!

Quartz, valued for its ubiquity and versatility, is the second-most-common mineral in Earth's crust. Its natural form yields gems like amethyst and citrine, while its synthetic form finds use in various electronic devices. The precise arrangements of its atomic building blocks—silicon and oxygen—result in the distinctive hexagonal prisms of quartz crystals.

Jeffrey Post, the Smithsonian's mineralogist, emphasizes the rarity and importance of the Berns Quartz. Its display not only showcases the marvels of the natural world but also fosters appreciation for Earth's geological wonders and their scientific significance. As visitors marvel at the Berns Quartz, they are invited to explore the beauty and scientific marvels of quartz crystals and the world they inhabit.

Photos courtesy of Sarah Wolven and Ron Coleman Mining

"SECRET" TUNNELS

Did the gangsters use tunnels underneath downtown to get around discreetly?

Legend has it there is an underground tunnel (running west to east under Central Avenue) linking the Arlington to the Southern Club and built by Al Capone, who would use it to secretly get around during his time here.

There is a tunnel that runs under Central Avenue and then the sidewalk in front of Bathhouse Row and eventually to Transportation Plaza. Hot Springs Creek runs through this tunnel, which is used for flood control.

Despite footage of various explorers making their way through the tunnel system found online, the national park does not recommend touring the tunnel due to safety hazards. In recent years, a A sign has now been put up warning, "DO NOT ENTER.

Starting at Whittington or Park Avenues at the north end of Central Avenue and ending at the Hot Springs Creek Greenway Trail, anyone touring may feel like they're in a dangerous territory of history, for more reasons than an imposing fall hazard. Are they stepping foot where an infamous gangster

TUNNEL ENTRY

WHAT: See the entry to the tunnels running under downtown Hot Springs for yourself.

WHERE: 811 Park Ave.

COST: Free

PRO TIP: Don't slip trying to see the inside!

> "This is a story that you can't beat to death with a stick—wish I could. One hundred percent this is not true."—Garland County Historical Society Executive Director Liz Robbins, 2024.

once hid? And will they find a "mysterious" bowling alley said to be in the tunnel(s)?

Could a tunnel have been secretly built underneath and perpendicular to the one you're able to access?

This tale of one or two tunnels used by Capone is widely believed locally and beyond, but it has little truth to it. From the knowledge I was able to acquire, there is only one tunnel, and that one was (and still is) used only by maintenance workers. There are access points throughout the tunnel, and that is the source of the bowling alley myth, Robbins said. An access for workers to the tunnel existed in a hotel's basement, which had a small bowling alley.

The less thrilling truth behind the inception of the tunnel is that it was built in 1884 by the US government.

"The work was directed by Samuel Hamblen, so the tunnel was then known as Hamblen's Arch," Robbins said. "The tunnel solved several problems. It provided flood control and also eliminated the need for bridges to connect bathhouses to the main street. The tunnel also got rid of an open creek, which held sewage, stones, staves, planks, bottles, and other trash."

IN THE GUTTER

Where is the abandoned bowling alley?

The small, abandoned bowling alley that has an access point to the aforementioned tunnel is in the basement of the Dugan-Stuart Building. That doorway's only purpose is to provide city maintenance with a more convenient route to sections of the tunnel. The alley is not visible or accessible to anyone touring the tunnel. However, there are rumors of bowling alleys easily mixed up in present-day local lore because downtown has not one but two abandoned bowling alleys.

LET'S BOWL

WHAT: Central Bowling Lanes

WHERE: 3917 Central Ave.

COST: About $10 a game.

PRO TIP: Games are half-price Sundays from 4 p.m. to close and Wednesdays from 6 p.m. to close.

The alley in the Dugan-Stuart Building was four lanes and included a pool room. It was first listed in a 1908 city directory under the name McRoberts Bowling Alley. After a 1923 flood destroyed the alley, it wouldn't be until 1930 that it was reopened as Royal Bowling Alleys under a different owner. The last documentation of Royal Bowling Alleys being in operation is in a 1938 *Sentinel-Record* ad. All that's left of the bowling alley today is an old scoreboard with names and scores intact.

This is not the same bowling alley featured in the widely shared photo of an abandoned downtown alley that fascinates urban explorers today. Many mistakenly believe that image depicts the old Royal Alleys. In reality, it shows a bowling alley once used by the Army and Navy General Hospital. While Royal Alleys was known as a hub for betting, the hospital's alley appears to have catered to a more "clean-cut" crowd.

In a December 1, 1951, issue of the *Bugle*, a publication for the Army and Navy General Hospital post, there are two sections titled "Meet the Team" and "Ten Pin Alley News." A

Photos courtesy of Michael Schwarz

photo of a sharply dressed man completing a graceful delivery of a ball down the alley is printed along with the article.

Although this alley is pretty well intact today, complete with a few stray bowling balls, pins, and shoes lying among the rubble, it is a hazard to step foot in. The former hospital campus is now also closed to visitors.

Earl Gill told the *Sentinel-Record* in 1988 he earned a nickel a line for setting pins at Royal Alleys. "My first day to work I made 15 cents and the second day I made 75 cents," he said. "It was a living."

CHARM OF THE MALL

What happened to the Hot Springs Mall?

Granted it's still open at the time of this book's publishing, if you go to Uptown Hot Springs today, you will see a fluorescent-lit, carpeted, mostly empty shell of a shopping mall. And if you're calling it by its newest name, Uptown Hot Springs, rather than the Hot Springs Mall, it's likely you weren't here to see the mall in its heyday.

Opened March 3, 1982, by Aronov Realty Co., the Hot Springs Mall was anchored by three major department stores: Dillard's, JCPenney, and Sears, along with 43 smaller stores. It provided around 800 jobs.

The Hot Springs Mall used to be a place of gathering. Longtime community members remember it fondly today.

"We used to walk from the skating rink to the mall for Corndog 7. Then go to the movies," Tyler Draper said.

"Each year the grade schools would decorate giant cardboard Easter eggs and they'd hang them along the walls and do a contest," Livvey Rurup III said. "Some of the stores would have their new seasonal lines debuted by local teenagers. . . . They'd put up catwalk-like stages."

"I'm old enough to remember when Chick-fil-A was still in the HS Mall," Jim Miller said. "Also, who could forget KB Toys and Waldenbooks? And, of course, Romancing the Stone! Teenage date nights and El Chico's chips and salsa. Man! The nostalgia reeks!"

"There wasn't anything you couldn't find at the mall," Tina Crump said. "Between the full stores, mini markets in the

---

"In the early 2010s, every Facebook post of mine was asking my friends if they were going to be at the mall that day," Amanda Albrecht said.

middle, advertising cars, Santa and the Easter bunny events, several community events throughout the year . . . there was always something new to see and something going on."

The mall still stands today with few stores and eateries. The independently owned movie theater, Hot Springs 8 VIP Cinema, located behind it, has been doing well for itself with remodels and expansions. Purchased by RockStep Capital on August 12, 2015, the mall was rebranded as Uptown Hot Springs in 2021. UHS has expressed that it would like to shy away from retail and include more entertainment-based businesses. Locals hope for the best in order to save their mall, preserving the memories within it.

VISIT THE MALL

WHAT: Spend a day visiting the shops left in the mall.

WHERE: 4501 Central Ave.

COST: Ranges. (Support these businesses!)

PRO TIP: Plan a day to spend at the mall, and catch a movie at the cinema afterward.

THEY BATHED THE WORLD

Who bathed the world?

The Black history on Bathhouse Row is deeply rooted and complex, but historians from the National Park Service have worked to help tell that history to the world today.

In collaboration with the community, park archeologist Victoria Reichard, park museum curator Tom Hill, and park ranger Daniel Chmill have gathered historical archives and oral histories to illustrate who bathed the world. Hill says there is so much of the story that has gone untold.

"It [working in the bathhouse] was a wonderful life for Black people, even in the Jim Crow South," Hill said. "They could make a good living, even compared to what White men and White women were making at the time.

"It's just if they wanted to do shopping or they wanted to do business, there were still restrictions on society. So they could work on Bathhouse Row, they could have patrons ask for them by name every year when they came back to bathe again and again in the bathhouses, but if they

THE UNTOLD STORIES

WHAT: Visit the Fordyce Bathhouse to learn more about the Black history behind the foundation of Hot Springs's beloved Bathhouse Row.

WHERE: 369 Central Ave.

COST: Free

PRO TIP: Visit theuzuriproject.org for more information on local Black history preservation.

Hot Springs National Park's Bathhouse Row has historically marketed itself with the slogan "We bathe the world," but few have stopped to think: *Who bathed the world?*

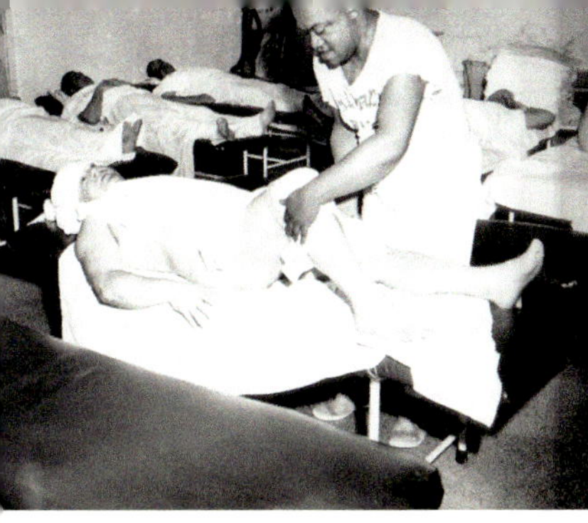

Photos courtesy of Hot Springs National Park

wanted to go out to eat or go to a bar or go shopping, they had to go to Black businesses because everything else was still racially segregated. And we don't talk about that in the park. We don't talk about the stories that are uncomfortable."

Hill said that more of an effort should be made in getting this story across to the visitors.

During Reconstruction, a Black man named A. C. Page briefly owned a bathhouse on Bathhouse Row. However, in the post-Reconstruction Jim Crow era, segregation became prevalent again, limiting the access of African Americans to bathhouses, although they still worked in most of them.

Liz Robbins notes that African Americans were allowed to take thermal baths in the Government Free Bathhouse. In 1905, the African American Crystal Bathhouse opened on Malvern Avenue. After it burned in 1913, it was replaced by the Pythian Bathhouse. African Americans could also bathe at the Woodmen of Union Hotel and Bathhouse (later the National Baptist Hotel and Bathhouse) on Malvern.

HELEN KELLER

What was Keller's business with Hot Springs?

Helen Keller excelled in every way in her 87 years of life, and anyone who had the chance to encounter her on her travels was lucky.

And it just so happens that Hot Springs was lucky enough to host Keller at least three known times during her lifetime. Her first visit was in May 1894, when she was 13 years old. She and her famous teacher Annie Sullivan came to Hot Springs to visit Keller's aunt and uncle, who had relocated to Hot Springs in 1877. Her uncle, Dr. James Keller, was a popular doctor and Confederate general in the community.

After her uncle's passing, Keller returned to Hot Springs two more times for work.

On March 25, 1916, Keller delivered a speech titled "Happiness" to the community during an appearance at the Auditorium Theater. Although there were no found reports of her speech's contents, the subject was one Keller often spoke on. Some of my favorite words from Keller on the subject are:

"When one door of happiness closes, another opens; but often we look so long at the closed door that we do not see the one which has been opened for us."

The final time Keller came to Hot Springs was in November 1944, visiting the Army and Navy General Hospital and a Hot Springs National Park Rotary Club luncheon. In a June 4, 1960, article from the *Sentinel-Record*, Hot Springs citizen

HELEN KELLER HISTORY

WHAT: A small tidbit of Keller's history at the Army and Navy General Hospital is retold in the Haunted Walking Tour.

WHERE: 430 Central Ave.

COST: Ticket price varies

PRO TIP: Visit the Helen Keller Archive at afb.org to explore speeches she gave around the country.

Photos courtesy of American Foundation for the Blind, Helen Keller Archives

Milton Nobles was quoted saying, "Miss Keller placed the fingers of her left hand on my lips while Mrs. Macy held Keller's right hand. When I completed my remarks of welcome to Hot Springs, thanking Miss Keller for attending the Rotary luncheon, her beautiful face lighted up with a warm smile and she gave her reply through Mrs. Macy's hand contact."*

**Although Nobles states in the 1960 article that Keller made this visit "around 1929," other reports show that the year was 1944.*

Keller became the first deaf/blind graduate of Radcliffe College of Harvard University, advocated for schools for the blind, cofounded the American Civil Liberties Union, and was an early proponent of the NAACP and birth control.

SO MANY OPEN HOUSES

Which abandoned building was renovated into a temporary art exhibit?

In September 2009, local nonprofit Low Key Arts thought outside of the box when it came to showcasing the beauty of abandoned ruins.

So Many Open Houses emerged as a unique site-specific art exhibit, transforming the raw interior of the Mountainaire—an abandoned hotel located at 1100 Park Avenue—into a canvas for creative expression.

Featuring a series of miniature open houses, artists navigated plaster walls and multiroom suites to bring their visions to life. What set this exhibit apart was its nonjuried nature, welcoming all forms of media and encouraging artists to break free from traditional constraints.

Artists, drawn to the unconventional venue, submitted their top-three space requests and conceptual descriptions. The

So Many Open Houses left an enduring legacy, showcasing the power of art to breathe life into forgotten spaces and communities.

CHECK OUT LOW KEY

WHAT: Low Key Arts continues to offer countless unique community events for artists and art lovers alike.

WHERE: Visit lowkeyarts.org

COST: Ranges

PRO TIP: Be sure to check out one of its hottest annual music festivals, Valley of the Vapors.

Photos courtesy of Aaron Brewer

resulting installations ranged from site-specific works to avant-garde sound, video, and performance pieces. One of the most iconic pieces displayed was a flight of stairs covered in hair. "Hairy Staircase" by Jessica Wohl garnered international attention.

"Despite the structure's disrepair, this work makes visible the tiny pulse I imagine coursing through its veins," Wohl said in her artist statement. "By creating a staircase of cascading hair, I imply that this building not only retains the energy of its former inhabitants but that it transforms that energy into a symbol of growth. I personify the hotel and imagine that it is still alive."

The Mountainaire Hotel played a pivotal role in the exhibit. Built in 1947 as a tourist destination, it later served as apartments and a nursing home before falling vacant in the mid-1990s. By 2007, it earned a spot on the Historic Preservation Alliance of Arkansas's list of Most Endangered Places. *So Many Open Houses* aimed to present the Mountainaire in a positive light, fostering a newfound appreciation for the abandoned ruins among the community.

COOPER JACK

Who was the homeless man always dressed in a suit walking the streets?

Every community has local staples who, when gone, are oftentimes remembered as community drivers for their financial, vocal, and/or compassionate contributions to the community. Hot Springs has a lot of these people, some of whom are mentioned throughout this book. But there is one local man who left a mark on the masses with his existence alone. Allow me to introduce you to the late Cooper Jack (also known as "Coopa Jack" or "Kooba Jack").

Killed in the daylight of August 2, 2022, by a driver while he was crossing the road between Crosswalk Bar and Oaklawn Racing Casino Resort, Cooper Jack was a man who left a legacy that shines a light on the complexities of human existence, the struggles of addiction, and the vibrant individuals who inhabit the streets.

Known for his impeccable attire, grasp on the bottle, and enigmatic persona, this nomadic man was loved by some and disregarded by others. But there was no denying the impact he had on the flavor and character of Hot Springs.

Throughout the years, rumors circulated about Cooper Jack's past, speculating that he had been a former pimp who migrated from Memphis. These speculations, along with his mysterious name and distinctive fashion sense, captivated the

THE MAN, THE MYTH, THE LEGEND

WHAT: An uncommon legacy left

WHERE: As of 2024, a memorial for Cooper Jack is located at 2714 Central Ave.

COST: You can make monetary donations to local organizations like Samaritan Ministries and the Jackson House.

PRO TIP: Monetary, food, and tarp donations can also be made to local organizations like Full Circle Missions and the Salvation Army.

Photo courtesy of Robbie Brindley

public's imagination and fueled countless theories. But in death, his older sister Betty Young was able to fill in some of the blanks while also illustrating the person behind the mystery.

Cooper Jack, whose real name was Donald Ray Thompson, was born in Hot Springs on January 17, 1958. After he completed school, his family moved to Memphis, but he returned to Hot Springs in the late 1980s. His nickname came from his brother Curtis when Thompson was 10 years old. He was an incredible artist and had dressed to the nines since he was young.

The loss of Cooper Jack left a void in the community, but his unique style, mysterious past, and undeniable presence will forever be etched in the memories of those who encountered him on the streets of Hot Springs. His story serves as a poignant reminder to embrace compassion and understanding for all individuals, regardless of their circumstances.

Aside from his dapper dress, another distinguishable trait of Cooper Jack was his love for fried chicken (or, as he called it, "yard bird"). One night while being patted down by police—not an uncommon occurrence for the Jack—the only thing found inside the pockets of his pink two-piece suit were numerous unwrapped pieces of chicken.

MAYBERRY SPRINGS

What happened at Mayberry Springs Inn?

The story of Mayberry Inn is a classic tale of a "haunted house" most avoided and rascals sought out, but the story has been at risk of extinction since the inn's burning in 2001. Everyone loves a good haunted house, and this area near Hot Springs had one that takes the cake. The Mayberry Springs Inn was built near Crystal Springs beside the road between Hot Springs and Mount Ida in the 1860s by a man named David Mayberry.

According to Larry Rhodes in an article for the Garland County Historical Society *Record*, here are the rumors surrounding the life and legacy of David Mayberry:

In the 1830s, Mayberry moved to Arkansas from Tennessee in an effort to run from the law after killing a man. In the 1850s, he was able to purchase the land that Mayberry Springs Inn would stand on with an inheritance from his father. He was settled in the house with his family at the time the Civil War began, which he fought in and during which he was shot 16 different times. Doctors were unable to remove all the bullets, and this is said to have taken a toll on Mayberry's sanity over time due to lead poisoning.

After the war, Mayberry ran the inn with his family. Running this popular destination for freight wagons and coaches was a lucrative career, yet the area was dangerous. Rhodes said his grandfather, who was raised near the inn, told of several men who had been murdered by outlaws raiding the place. But Mayberry only saw the inn as his own good fortune

MAYBERRY SPRINGS INN

WHAT: Haunting mystery

WHERE: It was located off Highway 270, near Crystal Springs.

COST: Free

PRO TIP: The inn is no longer there to visit, but the haunted highway is.

Photo courtesy of the Garland County Historical Society

and planned to use the rest of his land to expand and create a community. However, by the late 1870s, his mental health was in decline. Mayberry married his third wife in 1880 and died in 1881.

"It was said that Mayberry was an 'infidel' and that as he lay on his deathbed, chains could be heard rattling," Rhodes wrote. "It was whispered that he had murdered one of his wives and burned her body in the fireplace! There were said to be bodies of tortured slaves buried under the house, and the ghost of a headless man haunting the 'lobby' of the stagecoach inn."

But these stories turned into a haunting reality in the 1890s after the Rector family purchased the inn.

"Caretakers would sometimes see or hear things which made the long winter nights uneasy," Rhodes said. "One of the caretakers reported seeing a dead body inside the locked house, only to return and find the body gone! Louis Goodman, whom my grandfather trusted with the truth, said that while he was living in the caretaker's cabin (ca. 1916) he could hear someone shouting 'Help, Help!' and fiddle music and laughter from the inn's darkened rooms, becoming silent once a lantern was lit."

In 2009, a fire burned down the inn, leaving only the front steps, fireplace, and back building. I am unsure of accuracy and truth of these haunting stories, but as someone who has been on these grounds, I can confirm that the land and its remains are 100 percent spooky.

BLACK BROADWAY

Who contributed to Hot Springs's "Black Broadway"?

Of all the famed people who frequented Hot Springs, there is an extensive history of famous Black musicians coming out of Hot Springs.

Among these hidden gems is Henry Glover, a wiz in songwriting, arranging, producing, and trumpet playing. Raised in Hot Springs and the rural surroundings beyond town, Glover's diverse musical palette thrived. A prodigy in handling country, blues, pop, R & B, jazz, and rock 'n' roll, he became a sought-after arranger and talent scout. He produced records for artists ranging from country stars like Grandpa Jones to R & B icons like James Brown and early rock 'n' roll pioneers Levon and the Hawks.

Junius "Junie" Cobb, a Hot Springs native and jazz instrumentalist, possessed a virtuosity spanning various instruments. Starting as a pianist in Johnny Dunn's Band, he later led his own ensemble in Chicago, leaving an indelible mark on jazz with his prowess on reed instruments and piano.

CELEBRATE THE CULTURE

WHAT: Black Broadway mural

WHERE: 350 Malvern Ave.

COST: Free

PRO TIP: Some of these musicians can be seen in the Arkansas Walk of Fame located in front of the visitor center in downtown Hot Springs.

These musical maestros deriving from Hot Springs showcase the town's varied musical heritage.

Photo courtesy of Sherry Glover

John Marshall Greer, a blues tenor saxophonist and vocalist from Hot Springs, found his roots intertwined with Glover's at Alabama A&M. Joining Lucky Millinder's band on Glover's recommendation, Greer's career soared with hits like "Got You on My Mind" and the timeless Christmas classic "We Wanna See Santa Claus Do the Mambo."

Louis Jordan, although born in Brinkley, Arkansas, launched his national career in Hot Springs. Revered as the "father of R & B," Jordan's innovative style with his Tympany Five set the stage for the rock 'n' roll explosion. Playing at the Belvedere and other Hot Springs clubs, Jordan's influence rippled through the industry, shaping the sounds of Ray Charles, B. B. King, James Brown, and Chuck Berry.

OUR NATIVES

What's the real story behind the Native Americans who settled here?

Hot Springs's early promoters claimed that the land around the thermal springs was "neutral land" to which Native Americans of many tribes would come and, laying down their weapons, enjoy the healing waters. The early ads for Hot Springs said that the Native Americans had called it the "Valley of Peace." In 1541, according to other stories, Hernando de Soto was one of the first European colonizers to come here, which would have made it a far less peaceful valley. But this is all just the . . . lore.

Mark Blaeuer, a historian and former Hot Springs National Park Ranger, sets the record straight with the real history of Native Americans settling here in his book *Didn't All the Indians Come Here? Separating Fact from Fiction in Hot Springs National Park*. A book that pays respect to the reality

Original painting by Alison Parsons

of the first people to come to Hot Springs, it's the seldom-told story of the first settlers.

"The first Americans in Arkansas arrived by 9500 BC," Blaeuer writes. "Over the next ten thousand years, as their population grew, their descendants settled into smaller territories."

Blaeuer notes that by around 800 AD, Caddo tribes inhabited this region, having developed from earlier groups.

"Prehistoric American Indian sites do exist in the Hot Springs area," he writes. "On the other hand, there is no archaeological evidence for people using the hot springs thousands of years ago, although they may have done so."

In 1878, A. Van Cleef wrote that artifacts had been found in the "neighborhood" of the hot springs, but Blaeuer points out that that is too vague.

"It may, for instance, have meant as far away as Indian Mountain, three miles off but renowned by that time for its geological resources," he writes. "Moreover, the mere presence of artifacts nearby would not have proven that the springs were used, and certainly not how."

Furthermore, Blaeuer notes in his book it was not the custom for Native Americans to travel long distances away from their home territories to find medical relief.

QUAPAW MURAL

WHAT: A mural painted by Italian artist Pepe Gaka.

WHERE: 502 Central Ave.

COST: Free

PRO TIP: Although currently out of print, visit the Garland County Historical Society for reference copies of Blaeuer's book, *Didn't All the Indians Come Here?*

"Nevertheless, the fact remains: no unambiguously bathing-related prehistoric artifacts have ever been found."—Mark Blaeuer, *Didn't All the Indians Come Here?*

LET'S GET SALTY

Have you ever turned to salt for therapy?

Discover the transformative experience of the Salt Room at the Electric Strawberry in Hot Springs. Known as halotherapy, this holistic practice replicates the healing microclimate of salt caves. Inhaling micro-sized salt particles deeply penetrates the respiratory system, targeting ailments from asthma to allergies by combating inflammation and eliminating bacteria.

At the Electric Strawberry, guests unwind in a serene environment, enhancing relaxation with optional color therapy and even a Silent Disco option, where participants groove to music through headphones amid therapeutic salt particles. This innovative therapy detoxifies the body, restores balance, and bolsters immunity, promoting overall well-being.

The process involves dispersing salt particles less than three microns in size into a specially designed room using a halogenerator, ensuring optimal antibacterial effects and moisture reduction in airways and on skin. Widely recognized in Europe, halotherapy is integrated into healthcare systems and covered by insurance, reflecting its efficacy and safety.

For those seeking lasting benefits, regular sessions are recommended, with frequency tailored to individual health goals.

Whether aiming to manage chronic conditions or enhance general wellness, the Salt Room at the Electric Strawberry offers a natural, rejuvenating solution backed by scientific research and global wellness standards.

THE SALT ROOM

WHAT: A new kind of wellness

WHERE: The Electric Strawberry, 500 W Grand Ave.

COST: Ranges

PRO TIP: Don't just stop at salt therapy. Take advantage of the Electric Strawberry's full moon meditations, book club, and their apothocary/coffee shop/ book store/art gallery up front.

FINE DINING AND BREATHING

Where is the finest dining in all the land?

Tucked away within the Oaklawn Racing Casino Resort, the OAK room & bar is a hidden gem in Hot Springs. This fine dining establishment, often overlooked by those who don't frequent casinos, offers an exceptional culinary experience that stands out in the area.

The atmosphere at the OAK room & bar exudes elegance and romance. With its soft lighting, comfortable seating, and stylish decor, the space feels both intimate and luxurious. It's an ideal spot for a quiet evening where you can unwind and enjoy quality time with your companion. The staff's attentive service further enhances the experience, making each guest feel special.

The menu at the OAK room & bar is a true delight. The chefs use top-quality ingredients to create dishes that are as visually appealing as they are delicious. From perfectly cooked steaks to fresh, flavorful seafood, the food is prepared with great

care and skill. An extensive wine list and expertly crafted cocktails complement the meal, ensuring a perfect pairing for every dish.

For those looking to celebrate a special occasion or simply enjoy an extraordinary night out, the OAK room & bar offers a dining experience like no other in Hot Springs. It's a place where you can escape the usual casino atmosphere and savor an evening of fine food and romantic ambiance, creating memories that will last long after the meal is over.

OAK ROOM

WHAT: The best fine dining in town

WHERE: Oaklawn Racing Casino Resort, 2705 Central Ave.

COST: $$$

PRO TIP: Call ahead to make reservations.

Look for the astounding quartz centerpieces on some of the tables. They are Arkansas-grown works of art!

Photos courtesy of Oaklawn Racing Casino Resort

THE RESERVE

But where should I stay?

The secret is out on the best fine dining, but what about the best lodging? Located just across the street from Oaklawn, you will find an unforgettable bed-and-breakfast getaway in the Reserve at Hot Springs. This elegant historical estate presents a modern twist on Southern hospitality, offering a luxurious retreat in the heart of Hot Springs. Perched on four expansive acres of picturesque land, the Reserve boasts 12 beautifully appointed guest accommodations spread across the main Brown House, the adjacent Legacy House, and a private Cottage Suite.

The Reserve at Hot Springs engages all your senses, from the stunning sights of the property to the touch of luxury linens, the taste of renowned cuisine, and the attentive service. Each corner of the estate is designed to provide a serene escape from the daily hustle. Picture yourself lounging

THE RESERVE

WHAT: Best bed-and-breakfast in town

WHERE: 2330 Central Ave.

COST: $$$

PRO TIP: Look into the packages offered by the Reserve to make your Hot Springs visit complete with fun activities like boating the lakes.

Photos courtesy of the Reserve

on the charming swing by a tranquil waterfall, warming up by the outdoor firepit, or enjoying a bourbon in the cozy, wood-paneled library. These peaceful moments define the unique experience at this luxury hotel.

Guests at the Reserve are treated to top-notch amenities and exquisitely curated common spaces, making it the premier lodging choice in Hot Springs. Each morning begins with a complimentary breakfast, freshly prepared by executive chef Nathan McMurry, ensuring a delightful start to your day. Whether you're seeking relaxation or adventure, the Reserve at Hot Springs promises memories to last a lifetime.

The property's history and charm combined with modern luxury make it a standout destination. With every visit, guests are sure to discover new favorite spots, whether it's a quiet nook in the library, a sunny spot on the veranda, or a cozy seat by the fire. The Reserve at Hot Springs is more than just a place to stay; it's an experience that embodies the best of Southern hospitality, providing a perfect blend of comfort, elegance, and tranquility. For those seeking a truly special getaway, the Reserve is the ultimate choice.

Its central location makes it an ideal base for exploring the local attractions while enjoying a restful retreat.

So Many Open Houses
Photo courtesy of Aaron Brewer

SOURCES

Arkansas Democrat-Gazette

"Fans spot actor Liam Hemsworth in state as he films new movie directed by Arkansas native" by Tanner Newton / November 21, 2018

"Hot Springs' battles with blazes" by Tom Dillard / April 10, 2022

Books

Didn't All the Indians Come Here? by Mark Blaeuer: Chapter 3

Gambling in the Spa by Wayne Threadgill

Garland County, Arkansas: Our History and Heritage, edited by Isabel Burton Anthony: pages 33–34, 129, 201, 227

History of Townships 1880 by Inez E. Cline

Hot Springs Gunsmoke by Orval Allbritton: Chapters 11, 17

Indian Folklore Atlas by Marcus Phillips: pages 132–133

Leo and Verne by Orval Allbritton: pages 222–225, 275–277

Mob at the Spa by Orval Allbritton: Chapters 1, 5, 6

The Challengers: Untold Stories of African Americans Who Changed the System in One Small Southern Municipality by Elmer Beard: pages 1–9, 15–21

Then and Now: Hot Springs, Arkansas by Mike Blythe: page 88

Encyclopedia of Arkansas

"Army-Navy Hospital"

"Cheese Dip"

"Major League Spring Training in Hot Springs"

Other

Hot Springs Broadcast News Network / "Crazy Hot Springs street where your car seems to go uphill all by itself Gravity Hill" / Dec. 14, 2018, on YouTube

Low Keys Arts press release on "So Many Open Houses"

Radium Historical Items Catalog

"Bowling Alley" vertical file at the Garland County Historical Society

"Happy Hollow" vertical file at the Garland County Historical Society (Advertisement)

Other Articles

The Fog of Ward: "A Superman Mystery" by Dayton Ward / March 26, 2019

A Movie About Cheese Dip by Nick Rogers

A Superman "Mystery?" by Dayton Ward / March 26, 2019

Abandoned Arkansas: "Arbordale Fountain Lake" by Michael Schwarz / July 14, 2015

American Heritage / "The Double Life Of Hot Springs" by Wayne Fields / April 1991

Arcadia Publishing / *Louis Jordan: Son of Arkansas, Father of R&B* by Stephen Koch

Arkansas Catholic / "100 years later: Fact and legend on St. John Church in Hot Springs" by John Archibald / April 28, 2012

Arkansas Geological Survey (1984 Landslide)

Arkansas Historic Preservation Program: Butchie's Drive-In

Arkansas Tourism / Arkansas Cheese Dip Trail

Atlas Obscura: "Tiny Town"

Forbes / "A Haunted Hot Springs Comes Back to Life" by Regina Cole / Oct. 26, 2021

Hot Springs Natural / "History of Healing in Hot Springs, Arkansas" by Robert Pellegrino / January 12, 2021

Legal Defense Fund: Brown V. Board and "The Doll Test"

Ouachita Life / "Keller Connection" by Larry D. Rhodes / June 2009

Preserve Arkansas / "John Lee Webb House"

Smithsonian: "Massive Slab of Quartz Crystals Goes on Public View at Smithsonian" / Oct. 27, 2021

The Arkansas Art Scene Blog / "Interview with artist Longhua Xu" / Dec. 6, 2021

The Arkansas Times / "Hot Springs producer-songwriter Henry Glover wasn't just behind the scenes, he was inventing the scenes" by Stephen Koch / March 8, 2021

The Idle Class / "Translating a Heartbeat Through Technology" by Cassidy Kendall / Jan. 5, 2024

The Syncopated Times / "Junius Cobb"

THV11 / "Hot Springs has a steep landslide history" by Dan Grossman / March 26, 2014

Time / "Co-Founding the ACLU, Fighting for Labor Rights and Other Helen Keller Accomplishments Students Don't Learn in School" by Olivia B. Waxman / Dec. 15, 2020

The Hot Springs Post

"'Freedom' mural unveiled: designed to create hope, conversation as it neighbors Confederate Monument" by Cassidy Kendall / Nov. 20, 2021

"Black History in Hot Springs: Entertainers who came from the Spa City" by Cassidy Kendall / Feb. 23, 2022

"Black History in Hot Springs: Who bathed the world?" by Cassidy Kendall / Feb. 15, 2022

"Exploring cultural development in Hot Springs' recent art boon" by Cassidy Kendall / May 25, 2022

"How is climate change affecting the thermal springs?" by Cassidy Kendall / Aug. 25, 2021

"Local 'Barney' director, producer talks philosophy taught by purple dinosaur" by Cassidy Kendall / April 20, 2022

"Remembering 'Cooper Jack': The dapper man who made Hot Springs his home" by Cassidy Kendall / Aug. 6, 2022

"Sake Meets the South: Origami Sake to land in Hot Springs by end of year" by Cassidy Kendall / July 12, 2022

"The Policy Kings who came with the gangsters" by Cassidy Kendall / Feb. 8, 2022

"Who was Majestic Park driver Mike Dugan?" by Cassidy Kendall / Jan. 29 2022

"'Freedom mural' challenging downtown's confederate monument cut through for new restaurant" by Cassidy Kendall / Feb. 15, 2023

The Record

1981 / "Happy Hollow" by Jessie Gnatt Terry

1996 / "A City Drenched in Blood" by Orval Allbritton

2008 / "The Hot Springs Ostrich Farm" by Clyde Covington

2010 / "1895 Spa City Smallpox Epidemic" by Janis Percefull

2011 / "The Great Flood of May 14, 1923" by Robert Edward Reynolds

2017 / "Hot Springs Creek Tunnel Timeline" by Jerry Butler and Liz Robbins

2018 / "National Perspectives on Illegal Gambling and Corruption in Hot Springs" by Clay Farrar

2023 / "Dr. Mamie Phipps Clark: Hot Springs Hero Long Overlooked" by Tim Spofford

The *Sentinel-Record*
(Untitled) Sept. 5, 1961 (In the "Fires" vertical file at the Garland County Historical Society)

"Bombings remain mystery to this day" by Clay Farrar/ Sept. 26, 2018

"Breaking and entering, trespassing reported at former ACTI campus" by Cassidy Kendall, Jan. 4, 2021

Businessman relocates, says frustration is reason / Aug. 10, 2005

"Collisions Create Big Headaches for Tiny Town" by Max Bryan / July 7, 2016

"Couple to cap 17 years of Tesla Coil donations" by Cassidy Kendall / April 7, 2019

"Descendant: Death isn't 'ghost story'" by Max Bryan / Sept. 22, 2016

"Disaster brings out people's best, worst" by Melinda Gassaway / May 21, 1990

"Hell's Half Acre to heralded to visitors" / July 7, 1924

"HSNP to conduct guided hikes for Reservation Day" by Cassidy Kendall / April 8, 2021

"Melody in Glaze" by Cassidy Kendall / March 21, 2021

"New owner says mall will stay open, grow" by Don Thomason / Aug. 28, 2015

"Show Spotlights Hell's Half Acre" by Alison B. Harbour / May 1, 2010

"Spa City saw it all in the '80s" / Dec. 31, 1989

"Spa man recalls Keller visit to Hot Springs" / June 4, 1960

"Spa's downtown must change" / Date: unknown (In the "Pennington, Stueart '' vertical file at the Garland County Historical Society)

"Spooky Spa: Blade talks haunting of The Malco" by Cassidy Kendall / Oct. 30, 2020

"Spooky Spa: Unexplained happenings commonplace at Arlington" by Cassidy Kendall / Oct. 31, 2020

"Spooky Spa: 'Ghostplaces' scattered throughout the Ouachitas" by Cassidy Kendall / Oct. 23, 2020

"Spy Cats, Dolphins: Bailey trains thousands of animals" by Cassidy Kendall / March 24, 2019

"Sweet Chewaukla" excerpt from Sandra Long / Feb. 9, 1992

"Ties to Past / Human bones buried under church connect past, present" by Cassidy Kendall / Oct. 17, 2020

"Wednesday Night Poetry founder Kenny dies at 71" by Cassidy Kendall / Oct. 4, 2019

Websites
jessicawohl.com/work/mountainaire-hotel

sites.google.com/lowkeyarts.org/inceptiontoprojection

cityhs.net/697/City-Cemetery

findagrave.com/memorial/69133108/billy-ray-collins

flickr.com/photos/drmo/508115807

garvangardens.org

hotspringssistercity.org

nps.gov/hosp

sistercities.org

soest.hawaii.edu (quartz)

xu-longhua.com

Wikipedia
"Big John Greer"

"Bill Clinton"

"Daily Planet"

"Verna Cook Garvan"

"Gravity Hill"

Southern sake
Photo courtesy of Origami Sake

INDEX

De Soto

Cleansing Thermal Water